DRURY LANE PANTOMIME

THE WHITE CAT

THE WHITE CAT

WRITTEN & INVENTED BY
J. HICKORY WOOD & ARTHUR COLLINS

DRURY LANE PANTOMIME

Louis Wain

PUSS IN NEW BOOTS

Written by GEO. R. SIMS,
FRANK DIX & ARTHUR COLLINS. Produced by ARTHUR COLLINS.

DRURY LANE
PANTOMIME
MANAGING DIRECTOR ARTHUR COLLINS.

WRITTEN BY
ARTHUR COLLINS
AND FRANK DIX

THE BABES IN THE WOOD
PRODUCED BY ARTHUR COLLINS.

PANTOMIME:

By the same Authors

HAMLET THROUGH THE AGES

THEATRICAL COMPANION TO SHAW

THEATRICAL COMPANION TO MAUGHAM

THEATRICAL COMPANION TO COWARD

THE ARTIST AND THE THEATRE
(*The Story of the W. Somerset Maugham Theatrical Pictures*)

A PICTURE HISTORY OF BRITISH THEATRE

A PICTURE HISTORY OF OPERA
(*In collaboration with Philip Hope-Wallace*)

THE GAY TWENTIES
(*In collaboration with J. C. Trewin*)

THE TURBULENT THIRTIES
(*In collaboration with J. C. Trewin*)

THE THEATRES OF LONDON
(*Illustrated by Timothy Birdsall*)
(*Second edition revised in paper back*)

A PICTURE HISTORY OF GILBERT AND SULLIVAN

BRITISH MUSIC HALL, A STORY IN PICTURES

THE LOST THEATRES OF LONDON

MUSICAL COMEDY, A STORY IN PICTURES

REVUE, A STORY IN PICTURES

PANTOMIME

A STORY IN PICTURES

RAYMOND MANDER & JOE MITCHENSON

Foreword by DANNY LA RUE

'Pantomimes they never vary,
Every year the Prince, how dare he,
Woos and wins his Pickford, Mary.
Blast her godmother the Fairy!'
Douglas Byng

Taplinger Publishing Co., Inc.
New York

PRINCIPAL BOY

The Principal Boy
Was second to none,
A 'Romeo', 'Hamlet',
And 'Hotspur', in one;
Tragedy—comedy—
Farce or romance,
A voice for the singing,
And skill for the dance;
Cheeky and charming
With 'children-appeal',
To act the Old Stories
And make them seem real.

Gag with the Comics
And stooge for the Cat—
A popular ballad
Or something like that,
On a rickety beanstalk
Or wobbly wave,
Or chasing the spot-light
Round somebody's cave—
Climbing on rostrums
Of various heights
Up vertical ladders
In Palace-scene tights.

Down the Grand Staircase
Of steepness and dread—
Seven inch rises
And five inches tread—
A smile on the face
And a 'bride' by the hand,
Trussed like a turkey
And looking just grand.

These were a few things
She tackled with joy,
The truly invincible
Principal Boy.

First published in the United States in 1973 by
TAPLINGER PUBLISHING CO., INC.
New York, New York

Copyright © 1973 by Raymond Mander and Joe Mitchenson
All rights reserved.
Printed in Great Britain

Library of Congress Catalog Card Number: 73-6176
ISBN 0 8008 6233 3

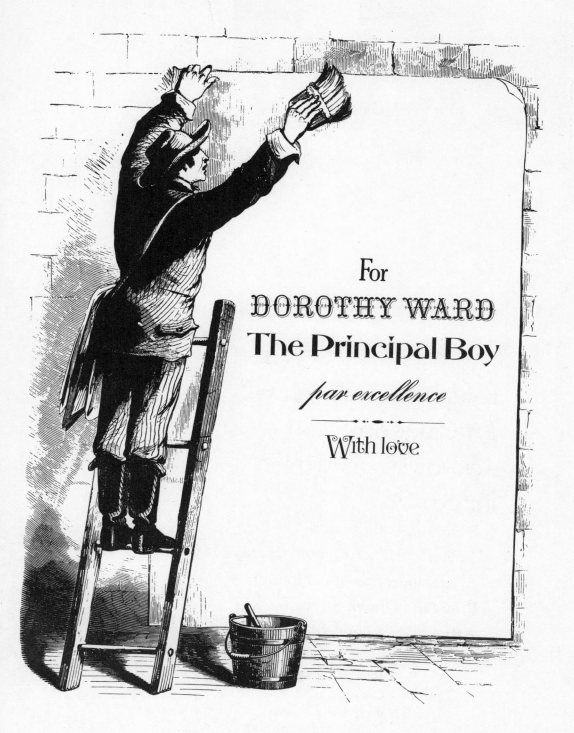

For
DOROTHY WARD
The Principal Boy
par excellence

With love

CONTENTS

Foreword by DANNY LA RUE

Dear Raymond and Joe,

I remember that when, some time ago, you were telling me about the progress of the work on this book, you said that your greatest problem was not what to put in, but what to leave out. Now that I see how widely and thoroughly you have covered the whole field of pantomime I understand what your problem must have been, and I am grateful and delighted that you have 'included me in' and not 'included me out'. As you know, pantomime has been a big part of my whole professional life, and I am quite sure that many of the happiest moments of my career have been in pantomime. I love it.

But of course you know that. We have often talked of those wonderful audiences. A pantomime audience is like no other theatre audience, yet all pantomime audiences seem to have something in common; the famed 'willingness to suspend disbelief' which is said to be the first essential to the creation of real theatrical magic.

Sitting in my dressing room, putting on my make-up before a pantomime performance, I am always waiting for the moment, just after the half hour call, when the first voices from the auditorium come echoing over the Tannoy. I have usually been aware of a steadily increasing level of noise around the outside of the theatre as the coaches arrive and the parties of excited kids mill around, laughing, or sometimes crying, and calling out to each other, or Mum or Aunty Glad, or the Sunday school teacher. Then come the first voices from inside the theatre, and for me the performance has already begun. More than any other, a pantomime audience is part of the show. The make-believe starts with them. Even days before as the grown-ups, perhaps a bit self-consciously, think themselves back into childhood as they prepare the youngsters for the planned treat. At a matinée, the noise in the theatre before the show can be so exciting that the whole cast gets a lift, and the rainy January afternoon disappears into the golden brightness of Panto-land even before the first cue floods the stage.

For me, the most rewarding times of all are the scenes I play on stage with children from the audience. I adore this. Some of the nicest compliments I have had as a performer have concerned this part of the show. The secret of success with children on stage is to treat them seriously as young people. I never try to put anything over on them, and I can usually gain their confidence by asking them to help me out. It is no use trying to be funny with children. If they have screwed up their courage to make that daunting journey from somewhere in the darkness on to the stage, it is because in some way or another they have become a part of the show and what is happening for them is, in current jargon, 'a valid and meaningful experience'. I try to take them a little further along with me, often by talking about their preparations for the trip. 'Is that a new frock for tonight? Did your mummy make it? Is it washable or do you send it to the dry cleaners?' and eventually, 'Now would you like to help me and all these other little boys and girls?'

Once the kids are talking about things they know and understand, that is the time when the real humour begins to come out of the situation. As when, you may remember, the young son of one of our best known musical comedy actresses, a pro to his finger tips and anxious not to let the side down, apologised because he couldn't sing the song but offered to tell a joke. I'll never forget the roar of laughter or the agony of his poor mum as he chanted with gusto 'There was a young man from Australia'.

A child's first visit to a theatre is usually to see a pantomime, and if one can produce the right kind of experience the theatre may gain a customer for life. With the witches and fairies and gnomes, the giants, the goose, the cat, beautiful princesses and handsome princes, wicked wizards, caves of jewels, palaces of gold, shipwrecks and adventures, pride humbled and virtue finally and trium-phantly rewarded, it is possible for a child with imagination to live through a kaleidoscope of emotions and laughter which may set him on a path to a lifetime of pleasure in the theatre.

Pantomime is indeed a thing to celebrate, and here you have recorded it and celebrated it beautifully. Thank you again and much success.

Sincerely,

Danny

The Story of Pantomime

THE BACKGROUND

Pantomime, like so many of our greatest national institutions, is a hybrid, created and understood only by the English! It takes its name from classical times and changes the meaning, its characters from Italian comedy and changes their names, its stories from continental fairy tales and mixes historical figures, then adds every conceivable trick and resource of the theatre, opera, ballet, music hall and musical comedy. It has moulded all these elements together over the past three hundred years into something which no-one but the English understand, or even want! Sufficient to say that the phrase 'a proper pantomime' means colloquially a state of utter confusion!

To sort out this confusion recourse to a dictionary is of little real help. In the *Shorter Oxford Dictionary* we read:

'PANTOMIME, from the Latin *pantomimus* one who plays a part in dumb show, a ballet dancer, a mimic.'

This is followed by:

'PANTOMIMUS, a Roman actor.'

Of him *The Oxford Companion to the Theatre* says:

'A performer popular in Imperial Rome, who by the use of movement and gesture, often stylized, represented in turn each character in a short scene based on classical history or mythology. He wore the costume of the tragic actor, a long cloak and silken tunic, but his mask, which was often changed for each rôle, had no mouthpiece. He was accompanied by musicians—usually flutes, pipes, cymbals, and trumpets—and a chorus, who sang in Greek the story which the actor was performing. (The most famous *pantomimi* were Pulades of Cilicia and Bathyllus of Alexandria, who played under Augustus, and Paris, put to death by Nero out of professional jealousy.) The art of the *pantomimus*, though considered by St Augustine more dangerous to morals than the circus, since it dealt exclusively with guilty passions and by its beauty and seductiveness had a disastrous effect on female spectators, was not, like its rival the Roman mime, coarse or vulgar.'

Next (quoting Grove's *Dictionary of Music*) *The Oxford Dictionary* adds:

'A kind of dramatic entertainment in which the performers express themselves by gestures to the accompaniment of music, and which may be called a prose ballet.'

Before going any further in their three-column entry, we cross-checked, and found:

'MIME, a mimic, jester, buffoon, a pantomimist' and 'a performer in dramatic pieces' which are described as 'a kind of simple farcical drama among the Greeks and Romans, characterized by mimicry and the ludicrous representation of familiar types of character; a dialogue written for recital in a performance of this kind. Also occasionally applied to similar performances or compositions in modern times.'

After this, like La Fontaine's Monsieur le Corbeau, we retired '*honteux et confus*', both for the lexicographer and ourselves! Then at last we found:

'An English dramatic performance, originally consisting of action without speech, but in its further development consisting of a dramatized tale, the *dénouement* of which is a transformation scene followed by the broad comedy of clown and pantaloon and the dancing of harlequin and columbine. Now a feature of the Christmas holidays.'

This is succinct but leaves out the contribution of burlesque and extravaganza (to be defined later in the right place), which were to add to the mixture to make Pantomime as we know it today.

There is no need to expand on the classical origins, except to note that it was an actor who gave pantomime its name.

The next and most important progenitor is *Commedia dell'Arte* or *Italian Comedy*, which also grew out of classical beginnings and survived the Middle Ages to flower in the Renaissance. Originally amateur, troupes played rustic comedies, remnants of the crude mimes of the Romans, at carnival time in southern Italy. Plays from these earlier days have survived and gradually, as professional groups were formed, they were to be found travelling all over Europe. They worked from a synopsis or scenario, not a complete text, improvising dialogue and 'business'. With each company the principal player had his own particular speciality or routine which could be introduced at will into any plot.

Each member had his or her own character or 'mask' and played nothing else —the old man, Pantalone, from which we get Pantaloon, the learned pedant (Il Dottore), the swashbuckling soldier (Il Capitano, the Dandy in embryo), the serving maids, and the comic servants. It was from among these last that the best-known survivals of the *Commedia dell'Arte* emerged, though very different from their originals. The Harlequin and Columbine of the English Harlequinade derive from Arlechino, via the French Arlequin, and Colombine: Punch (having vanished from pantomime to find immortality in the English Punch and Judy Show) from Pulcinella via the French Polichinelle and the early English Punchinello; Pierrot from Pedrolino; and the French comic characters Mezzetin, Scapin and Scaramouche (who never became acclimatized in England) from Mezzetino, Scapino and Scaramuccia.

Commedia dell'Arte companies settled in France from 1570, establishing a long tradition which influenced the comedies of Molière and Marivaux. Back in Italy the art declined, only to have a revival when Carlo Goldoni, in 1738, started to substitute completely written plays for the skeleton texts and the improvization. This did not succeed and the traditions were lost, although today we do occasionally see attempts to catch the forgotten magic. Strangely enough it was in English pantomime that some of the essential elements of *Commedia dell'Arte* survived longer than anywhere else.

In the sixteenth century, when *Commedia dell'Arte* was flourishing on the continent, Britain, hostile as ever to foreign customs and practices, did not take to the visits from troupes who made the Channel crossing, although at Court they received some appreciation.

In a painting by Marcus Gheraerts the Elder, a company is shown performing in full traditional style at Kenilworth Castle, in 1575, before Queen Elizabeth and her court. In this open-air performance, it is thought by the Gelosi company, and the first visit of *Commedia dell'Arte* to England, it is amusing to see they are accompanied by a Negro band of six musicians.

It must be remembered that women performed with these troupes, which may account for their rejection by the general public, with its 'puritan' mentality, which forbade women on the public stage until after the Restoration in 1660, in spite of the private experiments, made *sub rosa*, and these continental visitors.

Commedia dell'Arte, though, was to have its influence on English dramatists. Traces can be found in Shakespeare and the Jacobean playwrights, and Otway borrowed from Molière for his *Cheats of Scapin* in 1676; but it was left to John Rich, and a chain of circumstances, to acclimatize and assimilate the traditional characters into the British theatre and to give the meaning we now accept for the name pantomime—although it may have changed vastly since his day, and is often the opposite of the dictionary's definition!

THE LONDON STAGE

At the turn of the seventeenth century theatrical London was in revolt. The public, roused by Jeremy Collier in 1698, looking for a scapegoat on which to blame all the political and social troubles of the times, attacked the stage and its playwrights. Audiences were turning away from the permissive Restoration theatre to a more moral style of play and a pseudo-classical drama—often masking a political tract—designed for the new upper-middle-class audience which had joined the aristocratic frequenters of the playhouse of earlier times. Puritan middle-class morality was striving to raise its ugly head in much the same way as we are experiencing today when once again entertainment, now in a wider sense, is the target.

The theatre still operated under the two Patents granted by Charles II to Killegrew and the King's men and Davenant and the Duke's men. The former were housed, in 1674, in a new rebuilt Theatre Royal, Drury Lane, and the Duke's men were at the Dorset Garden Theatre. After a tussle and intense rivalry the two houses were united in 1682, but not for long. In 1690 the Davenant Patent was sold to a rascally lawyer, Christopher Rich, who mismanaged the theatre and angered the actors; another quarrel ensued, ending in Betterton, the leading actor of the day, returning, in 1695, to the old disused playhouse in

Lincoln's Inn Fields, and eventually to the new Queen's Theatre, in the Haymarket, which was built by Vanbrugh in 1705, though these activities were officially outside the Royal Patent.

The chaos and rivalry became worse, Rich was finally turned out of the Lane and the theatre was successfully taken over by three actors, Cibber, Doggett and Wilks, in 1711, working under Killegrew's Patent as a united company for drama, leaving the Queen's solely as an opera house, which it was to remain, with the addition of ballet, for over one hundred and fifty years.

Though peace had returned the drama was being heavily challenged at this time by the growth of the craze for Italian opera, which had ensnared the aristocratic playgoer. Even the managers of Drury Lane themselves had to pander to the fashion and produce opera as well as plays for their audience. The time was ripe for the introduction of a more popular entertainment for the less discerning playgoer.

Meantime the dispossessed Christopher Rich took over the empty Lincoln's Inn Fields Theatre (with, he claimed, the Davenant Patent) and started to rebuild it, but died before it was completed. John Rich took his father's place as manager and opened the theatre on 14 December 1714 with the usual dramatic entertainment and a company of actors not without distinction.

JOHN RICH

John Rich (he was born in 1692), had pretensions to being an actor, particularly in tragic rôles, but unfortunately he was totally unsuited for this kind of stage career. His detractors and jealous rivals, when he eventually made a success, were ready to put about stories to his detriment, and the stigma of illiteracy has long clung to his name.

His latest biographer, Paul Sawyer, (in a preliminary article published in *Theatre Notebook* in autumn 1972) says:

'That his contemporaries made numerous uncomplimentary observations upon his education and intelligence cannot be denied. Tate Wilkinson talked of his "*natural* stupidity", Charles Dibdin termed him "perhaps the most ignorant of all human beings", Aaron Hill in *The Prompter* asserted that Rich's "understanding was born deaf . . ." ' He continues, 'Thomas Davies, a less biased critic than many others, remarked that Rich's understanding was good, although because of a "grossly neglected" education his language was vulgar and ungrammatical.' Sawyer concludes, 'The most forthrightly damning, and perhaps the most influential verdict for our time, was the late nineteenth century one rendered by Joseph Knight in his *Dictionary of National Biography* article on Rich. He was, declared Knight, "quite illiterate".'

Once again, as we have so often found, the Victorian verdict or statement has been accepted by the modern encyclopaedists, the most recent *Concise Oxford Companion to the Theatre* is even more explicit and, as usual, piling wrong upon wrong dubs Rich '*completely* illiterate'. Paul Sawyer brings several strong pieces of contemporary evidence to disprove Knight's charge as well as a newly discovered letter, undoubtedly in Rich's own hand. As he says:

'The various inconsistencies and irregularities in punctuation, the occasional spellings and laborious phrases, . . . lend credence to my belief that this letter

[4]

is holographic, thus effectively destroying any statement impugning Rich's literacy.'

This new aspect of Rich helps towards a better understanding of his character and ambitions: a frustrated actor and a theatre manager with, as he must have realized, a gift for mime and above all the instinct and intuition which are to be found to this day in the successful purveyor of popular entertainment.

During the first decade of the century, when conditions allowed, French companies and actors from the fairs had regularly visited London, appearing at the theatres and the London fairs. These companies brought their own native version of Italian comedy which had been stabilized by Gherardi in his *Le Théâtre Italien* in 1700. It was their repertoires and their performers which both influenced and taught Rich and led the way to the development of our own particular brand of pantomime.

During 1716 John Weaver, a dancing master, staged at Drury Lane short ballets at the end of the plays, often called 'Italian Night Scenes', with the traditional *Commedia* characters. Rich copied these at Lincoln's Inn and, on 26 December 1716, 'performed for the first time' *A New Italian Mimic Scene between a Scaramouche, a Harlequin, a Country Farmer, his Wife and Others*, with himself (under the name of Lun) as Harlequin and John Thurmond as Scaramouche. This, by 29 January 1717, had become titled *Harlequin Executed; or, The Farmer Disappointed*, most likely indicating that the action was more English.

Later, on 2 March, Weaver staged at Drury Lane *The Loves of Mars and Venus*, 'A new Dramatic Entertainment of Dancing after the manner of the Antient Pantomimes', the first time the word pantomime was used with this meaning.

Weaver continued producing balletic entertainments with traditional themes at the Lane, sometimes appearing himself as Harlequin; but it was *The Cheats; or, The Tavern Bilkers* on 22 April at Lincoln's Inn that firmly placed Harlequin (Rich) in a contemporary London setting, and it was Rich who developed his own individual, less balletic, style of pantomime—the one which was soon to draw the town.

The development of stage machinery in the Restoration Theatre and its use in masques and operas had allowed any number of seemingly miraculous transformations and spectacles to be staged; also the popularity of conjuring tricks, presented by itinerant magicians at the London fairs, must have had their influence on a fertile mind looking for a means of self-expression and of making money. Rich had created for himself the character of Lun; with a harlequin mask to hide his plain features, and Harlequin's dumbness as a cover for his coarse speech; a disguise, maybe, to separate his own personality from his managerial position.

In the early days these entertainments were still advertised as being 'In the Italian Manner' and the story or legend used was interwoven with the adventures of Harlequin and his companions. It was this form that was adhered to by Rich and his followers, but later, as other writers and managers produced similar entertainments, a recognizable format for pantomime, as it soon became generally called, began to emerge. At the beginning there was an Opening, a familiar story or classical legend, told in verse and song, often burlesquing the current Italian opera. Then, by some invented benevolent agency, in early days usually a magician★ who thwarted the powers of evil, the characters were transformed into Harlequin, Columbine, Pantaloon, Punch, Pierrot, etc., who went through numerous tricks and adventures mimed to music, known as a Harlequinade. This often satirized the topical events of the day.

Rich's first outstanding success was with *The Necromancer; or, Harlequin Doctor Faustus*, produced in December 1723. Pantomime was being copied *à la Rich* even at Drury Lane, there they managed to stage a pantomime on a similar subject, by John Thurmond. A month earlier even the Little Theatre in the Haymarket, a Minor theatre, also played a version of the Faust legend. Being without dialogue it avoided the monopoly of the Patent theatres.

Although Rich engaged James Quinn as his leading dramatic actor in 1717, and he had established himself as one of the leading actors of the day, it was pantomime which helped fill the theatre, though as yet it was not irrevocably associated with the Christmas season and for children.

With Lewis Theobald in 1725 Rich devised *Harlequin Sorcerer with the Loves of Pluto and Proserpine*, another of his great successes, which was revived several times. When in 1752 Rich again put it on, 'with alterations', a full description of the action appeared in the *Gentleman's Magazine*:

'After the overture, as the curtain draws up, the first scene presents us with a group of witches exercising their orgies in a wilderness by moonlight. After a few songs, Harlequin crosses the stage, riding in the air between two witches upon a long pole, and jumps in among them.—Then you have a dance of witches, where you may be sure a proper use is made of their broomsticks.

'Next you see the bricklayers and their men going to work, which now marks the time of our drama to be morning. Harlequin then stands before a balcony, serenading Columbine, who appears to him; but, as he is climbing up, he is surpris'd by Pantaloon, who comes out opening the door, and Harlequin pops in. Hence a warm pursuit ensues of Columbine and our hero by Pantaloon and his servants. The next scene is of an house half built, with real scaffolding before it, and the men at work upon it. Columbine retires behind a pile of bricks: our hero mounts a ladder, and presently down comes the scaffolding with the men and all upon it.

'You next come to a garden wall: where, as Columbine retires under it, Harlequin is turn'd into an old woman, and the scene converted into a wall with ballads and coloured wooden prints strung upon it, with a large wicker chair, in which Harlequin seats himself, supposed to be selling them. The servant comes in, buys a ballad; and here a slight satirical hint is levelled at the song of "I love Sue, and Sue loves—" introduced in the rival *Harlequin Ranger* of t'other house.

'We have now a most delightful perspective of a farm-house, whence you hear the coots in the water as at a distance. Several rustics with their doxies come on; and Mr Lowe sings an excellent song, to which all join in chorus, to celebrate harvest home. This scene remov'd, a constable comes on, with the bricklayer's men, who have a warrant to take up Harlequin. Then you have a distant view of a barley mow and barn; several swains dancing before it, with Harlequin and Columbine. The constable and followers opportunely coming in, Columbine is seized and carried home by Pantaloon.

★ He was another form of the *Deus ex Machina* of the masques and operas and a relic of the Mystery and Morality plays when Good (on the right) and Evil (on the left) traditionally fought it out.

'When they are in the house, the servant after many dumb gestures introduces a large ostrich, which has a very good effect upon the audience; but perhaps would have had a greater, had we not discovered by the extremities, that it was Harlequin, whose legs and thighs appear under the body. This I suppose could not be remedied, as the extremities of this bird are very small in proportion. Besides, Columbine by this means discovers him; and, after having made the whole house ring with applause by playing several tricks, (such as kissing Columbine, biting the servant, and the like,) they morrice off both together.

'We are then carried to a back-part of the farm-house, which turns into a shed, where in an instant you have the view of a copper with a fire burning under it. Harlequin changes himself into an old washerwoman, and on striking a mound raised of flints mixed with earth, it is immediately turned into a washing-tub and stand; then opening a door, he shews us an horse with real linnen upon it, which is drawn out in many folds to a considerable length upon the stage. Pantaloon and servant come in, and after being soused with the soapsuds, are driven off by the supposed washerwoman with a bowl of boiling water from the copper, to the no small diversion of both galleries. Columbine then comes forth from her retreat, and goes off with her sweetheart.

'But the constable at last catches him; he tumbles down 'midst his guards, and slips away from 'em. We then see a fence of boards, as before a building, (excellently well painted,) which in a moment is converted to a gilt Equestrian statue. Harlequin is discovered to bestride the horse, as I remember by his sneezing; Pantaloon's servant goes to climb up by the head, which directly bends its neck and bites him: he next tries to get up by the hind-leg, which in springing back gives him a most terrible kick, and the poor dog is carried off with his face all over blood and beaten to pieces.

'After this, a scene drops, and gives us a prospect of ruinous rugged cliffs, with two trees hanging over them, beautifully executed. The same witches come in again, and, after singing a little while, retire. Then Harlequin appears disconsolate and prostrate upon a couch in an elegant apartment: lightning flashes; and four devils, in flame-coloured stockings, mount through trap-doors, surround him with double-tongued forks, and the whole stage with the scenery and all upon it, rises up gradually, and is carried all together into the air.

'Here the Pantomime ends; and the scrupulous critic must not nicely enquire into the reasons, why Harlequin is carried upwards into the infernal regions; nor why Pluto with his fair Proserpine descends in a magnificent throne afterwards, into a fine pavillion. After a song or two, an imp brings him word, that poor Harly is trapped at last; but the black-bearded monarch says, everything shall be jolly. Then the stage is extended to a prodigious depth, closing with a prospect of fine gardens and a temple. We are entertained a while with the agility of Mess. Cook, Grandchamps, Mademoiselles Camargo, Hilliard, and others; then with a grand chorus; lastly, with a low bow from the performers. And lo down drops the curtain.'

The Harlequin is not named, but could have been Rich, as he was still playing in the 1753 season. In his last years he grew corpulent, suffered from various ailments, and was going blind in one eye.

Throughout this era, certain successful scenes or pieces of 'business' were transplanted from pantomime to pantomime and remained in use over many years, becoming 'traditional' and establishing this much used adjective in association with pantomime.

Pantomime had now arrived. So far as the play-going public was concerned it was triumphant, to the intense disgust of the select few.

'See now,' cried Pope:

> 'See now what Dulness and her sons admire!
> See what the charms that smite the simple heart,
> Not touched by nature, and not reached by art.

★ ★ ★ ★ ★ ★

> Behold a sable sorcerer rise,
> Swift to whose hand a winged volume flies;
> All sudden, gorgons hiss and dragons glare,
> And ten-horned fiends and giants rush to war.
> Hell rises, Heaven descends; and dance on earth,
> Gods, imps and monsters, music, rage, and mirth,
> A fire, a jig, a battle and a ball,
> Till one wide conflagration swallows all.
>   Thence a new world, to Nature's laws unknown,
> Breaks out refulgent with a heaven its own;
> Another Cynthia her new journey runs,
> And other planets circle other suns.
> The forests dance, the rivers upward rise,
> Whales sport in woods, and dolphins in the skies;
> At last, to give the whole creation grace,
> Lo! one vast egg produces human race!'

This egg 'business' of Rich was the hatching of Harlequin by heat, described by one who saw it—an actor himself—as a masterpiece of dumb-show: 'From the first chipping of the egg, his receiving of motion, his feeling of the ground, his standing upright, to his quick Harlequin trip round the empty shell—through the whole progression every limb had its tongue, which spoke with most miraculous organ to the understandings and sensations of the observers.'

Looking back as people so often do to the lost days of their youth, an anonymous writer says:

'Rich's pantomimes, which were real pantomimes—that is, plays without words—consisted of two parts—one serious, the other comic; the first founded upon some old-world fable, between the pauses or acts of which were portrayed the trials and troubles of Harlequin and Columbine in their courtship; introducing a variety of surprising adventures, during which the magic bat of the hero was busy transforming palaces to huts, men to wheelbarrows, women to joint-stools, trees into houses, colonnades into tulip-beds, and other things into ostriches and serpents—the whole being set off with splendid scenery, handsome dresses, magnificent decorations, brilliant dances, and gay music. Flying cars and mechanical monsters were also among the prominent features of these strangely compounded dramatic entertainments. In *Orpheus and Eurydice*, Rich needed a super excellent serpent to kill Eurydice; and after some trouble, got

[8]

one made to his mind, which proved to be the public mind as well. The clever contriver of the reptile was so intoxicated with the success he had achieved that he devoted himself thenceforth entirely to serpents, for which he could find no market, and consequently found himself in the Bankruptcy Court—ruined by success.'

Henry Fielding was among Harlequin's detractors; he describes 'that most exquisite entertainment called the English pantomime [as] consisting of two parts: the serious portion exhibiting a certain number of heathen gods and goddesses, who were the worst and dullest company into which an audience were introduced; and—a secret known to few—were actually intended to be so, in order to contrast the comic part, and display the tricks of Harlequin to better advantage. The comic part being duller than anything before shown on the stage, could only be set off by the superlative dullness of the serious portion, in which the gods and goddesses were so insufferably tedious, that Harlequin was always welcome, by way of relief from still worse company.'

It must be remembered that Rich was an accomplished dancer 'who could scratch his ear with his foot like a dog and rapidly execute two or three hundred steps in an advance of three yards'. It is also said, 'His consummate skill in teaching others to express the language of the mind by action, was evident from the great number of actors he produced to fill up the unimportant parts of his mimic scenes.'

Once having struck gold, so to speak, with his Harlequin's magic bat, Rich went on to stage *The Beggar's Opera*, John Gay's satire both of political and operatic practices, which had been turned down by Drury Lane. This ran at Lincoln's Inn for a record of sixty-two consecutive performances and, dare we say it yet again, made 'Gay Rich and Rich Gay'!

With all this success Rich decided, in 1731, to build himself a new theatre; selecting a spot in Covent Garden he proceeded with the work. The Theatre Royal, Covent Garden, with the Davenant Patent, was opened on 7 December 1732, and the great rivalry of the two Royal houses began; a battle which was to last for over the next hundred years.

THEATRICAL RIVALRY

The Theatre Royal, Drury Lane, now had this extremely formidable rival nearby, and they themselves were again suffering internal dissention. By 1733 Colley Cibber was left in sole possession but sold out to his rascally son, Theophilus, leading to yet another revolt of the actors.

Fielding's political satires, both in word and mime, at the Little Theatre in the Haymarket, had drawn upon him the wrath of Sir Robert Walpole and caused the introduction of censorship, with the Licensing Act of 1737, confirming the monopoly of Drury Lane and Covent Garden under the Lord Chamberlain's jurisdiction.

The year before this there had been an attempt, in the House of Commons, not only to limit the playhouses but to restrain the 'licentiousness of the plays'. A satirical print, 'The Players' Last Refuge; or, The Strollers in Distress', is reproduced as picture 13. A fuller description of this print is here based on the information in the *British Museum Catalogue of Personal and Political Satires*.

The design represents a large open space, being Goodman's Fields, London, where stood a theatre, the property of Henry Giffard. In the centre of the open space is a half-ruined booth, such as was used for theatres. In front (1) in an attitude of great dejection, sits Theophilus Cibber (?), as Hannibal, in a 'Roman shape', with a very high helmet, a full-bottomed wig, buskins, etc. (2) A man in the dress of Harlequin (Lun, Rich the manager) stands in a hole, or grave, before Cibber, and appears to be endeavouring to soothe him by an offer of a mask and pistols, probably the weapons are intended to suggest suicide. (3) Two figures with a single number, Despair and Poverty, who stand by the side of Cibber's chair, the one half-naked and looking like a lunatic, the other miserable in appearance and clothed in rags.

The character of Hannibal is one of those in *Sophonisba; or, Hannibal's Overthrow*, a play by Nathaniel Lee which was revived at Covent Garden Theatre, for the benefit of Thomas Walker, on Saturday, 15 March 1735. In this case the part of Hannibal was played by Samuel Stephens, that of Sophonisba by Mrs Christopher Bullock.

(4) is Sophonisba, a young actress who holds a small covered pot, or noggin, in one hand, and a flask in the other; she is drinking Hollands in despair, and is characteristically dressed in a coronet and plume. (5) is Hob, digging a grave, and looking towards (6), the corpse of Pistol (Theophilus Cibber), which is borne on a bier by (a) Hamlet, an actor dressed in a long-skirted coat, a cocked hat with a feather trimming on its edges, a long wig, clock'd stockings, and shoes, (b) Falstaff, (Griffin or Harper), (c) Harlequin, with a laurel crown, and (d), as the text states, Orpheus, whose face is hidden, and who wears an embroidered surtout, knee-breeches, with rosettes, stockings and shoes. (7) and (7) are weeping and wiping their eyes. (8) shows Sir John Barnard mounted, and with sword drawn, riding down Punch, who is prostrate on the pavement; a man in a cocked hat overthrows a sausage and black-pudding stall, the female proprietor of which is wringing her hands in dismay. Behind the bier is borne a banner like that of a knight, and inscribed 'Pistol's no more.' In front lie a lantern (as in Hogarth's 'Southwark Fair') inscribed 'Lee and Harper' (the proprietors of a theatrical booth popular at the London fairs, such as St Bartholomew's and Southwark), a Roman eagle, coronet, turban, chain, battle-axe, goblet, shield, trumpet, quiver and tambourine, theatrical properties supposed to have become useless.

The earlier satires of Hogarth all show the popularity (or unpopularity, according to individual taste) of pantomime. Once dramatic censorship was introduced over the spoken word pantomime was more and more being used, as dumb show was not covered, to attack or satirize political or forbidden subjects. It could not be prohibited either at the Minor theatres like Goodman's Fields, where a turning-point of theatre history occurred on 9 October 1741. On that date David Garrick made his sensational début, a success which, incidentally, brought the wrath of the Patent Theatres on the head of Henry Giffard, who had until now quietly run his theatre unmolested. Here Garrick himself has been traditionally said to have played Harlequin in an emergency before he made his professional début. He was snapped up by Drury Lane when he first appeared in 1742; eventually, after a season with Rich at Covent Garden, he became manager of Drury Lane in 1747, where he remained until he retired in 1776.

Garrick initiated many reforms at the Lane. The behaviour of actors, the manners and customs of the audience and the staging of plays all received his attention. Originally he was against pantomime and, as he said, in the words of Samuel Johnson's prologue when he became manager:

'Hard is his lot, that here by fortune plac'd
Must watch the wild vicissitude of taste
With every meteor of caprice must play
And chance the new blown bubbles of the day.
Ah, let not censure term our fate our choice,
The stage but echoes back the public voice,
The drama's laws, the drama's patrons give
For we that live to please, must please to live.
Then prompt no more the follies you decry,
As tyrants doom their tools of guilt to die;
'Tis yours, this night, to bid the reign commence
Of rescued nature, and reviving sense;
To chace the charm of sound, the pomp of show
For useful mirth and salutary woe
Bid scenic virtue form the rising age
And truth diffuse her radiance from the stage.'

It is obvious that by 'the new blown bubbles of the day' he was having his dig at Rich and pantomime.

Yet Garrick was, by popular demand, forced to stage pantomime and by his genius managed to beat Rich at his own game. Covent Garden had been run in the ways of an older generation and Garrick brought more modern stage-craft to his aid.

On Boxing Day 1750, Garrick staged *Queen Mab*, 'an entertainment with Italian grotesque characters', with Henry Woodward as Harlequin. Woodward had been trained under Rich and had become known as 'Lun Junior'. He had appeared with Garrick in 1747 at Covent Garden and, after a spell in Dublin, where he staged a pantomime (later to become *Queen Mab*), he joined Garrick's company at Drury Lane where he became a favourite and accomplished actor. It was probably his insistence that at last persuaded Garrick to allow him to stage his pantomime, *Queen Mab*, or perhaps the wily manager took a common-sense view of business! He said in a prologue:

'Sacred to Shakespeare was this spot designed,
To pierce the heart, and humanise the mind,
But if an empty house, the actor's curse,
Shows us our Lears and Hamlets lose their force:
Unwilling, we must change the noble scene,
And in our turn present you Harlequin.'

The success of this departure is shown in the contemporary satire, 'The Theatrical Steel-Yard of 1750' (picture 14).

Theophilus Cibber in 1759 wrote a diatribe against the tastes of the day and Garrick in particular (a satirical engraving from this is picture 9). It was a case of Satan reproving sin, as Cibber had both concocted pantomimes and played Harlequin. He says:

'Let us then review the acting manager of Drury Lane. In the year 1747 Garrick opened that theatre with an excellent prologue; the conclusion of which gave the town to hope 'twould be their fault if, from that time, any farcical absurdity of pantomime or fooleries from France were again intruded on 'em . . . But has he kept his word during his successful reign? Has the stage been preserved in its proper purity, decency, and dignity? Have no good new plays been refused nor neglected? Have none but the most moral and elegant of the old ones been reviv'd? Have we not had a great number of these unmeaning fopperies miscall'd Entertainments, than ever was known to disgrace the stage in so few years? Has not every year produced one of these patch-work pantomimes?'

Queen Mab was revived (with alterations and additions) almost yearly until 1775. The next success, also by Woodward, was *Harlequin Ranger* in 1751, which held the stage until 1762. The greatest success of Garrick's management was *Harlequin's Invasion; or, A Christmas Gambol*, 'after the manner of the Italian Comedy', which he wrote himself with George Colman the elder. This opened, with Thomas King as Harlequin, on 31 December 1756. (King was to create Sir Peter Teazle twenty-one years later.) This pantomime was revived at the Lane many times and even reappeared at its old home in 1820. It was recalled by Charles Lamb from his childhood. In 'First Play' he says:

'*Harlequin's Invasion* followed, in which I remember the transformation of the magistrates into reverend beddams seemed to me a piece of grave, historical justice, and the tailor carrying his own head to be as sober a verity as the legend of St. Denys.'

W. J. Lawrence, the theatrical historian, says:

'This extraordinary pantomime was evolved by Garrick and the elder Colman, out of a slight burletta (*Harlequin versus Shakespeare*) which the former had written for a favoured performer at Bartholomew Fair. The plot of the Drury Lane production is not remarkable for its originality, and, indeed, smacks somewhat of the rehearsed tragedy in *Pasquin*, with this notable difference, that while in Fielding's memorable piece the triumph of Ignorance follows close upon the murder of Commonsense, the parti-coloured marauder and his satellites in *Harlequin's Invasion* are utterly routed and repulsed by the invincible Shakespeare. Just by way of novelty, Harlequin was for once endowed with the gift of speech; and Garrick, in referring to this retrogression in his prologue (spoken by King in the character of Harlequin), pays a graceful compliment to Rich:

> 'But why a speaking Harlequin?—'Tis wrong,
> The wits will say, to give the fool a tongue;
> When Lun appear'd with matchless art and whim,
> He gave the pow'r of speech to ev'ry limb;
> Tho' mask'd and mute, convey'd his quick intent,
> And told in frolic gestures all he meant.
> But now the motley coat, and sword of wood,
> Requires a tongue to make them understood.'

'King made', says Lawrence, 'an inimitable pattering Harlequin; Boaden tells us that "his saucy valets have never been approached"—high praise from such a critic! The comedian's reputation in this part became so great, that we find the *London Magazine* of February 1775 stating that the authors "are more indebted to the babylonish change of tongues in Tom King than to their wit, humour, or ingenuity: for in that scene harlequin assumes many dialects, but appears as ridiculous as we could wish him, when placed before the countenance of the immortal Shakespeare." A passage in King's letter to Garrick under date "Liverpool, 24 July, 1767," shows that other prominent actors had been associated with this famous pantomime at an early period:

' " As to *The Invasion*, I think it would be proper that I should keep my part, and Parsons be put into Snip. Should Yates think better of it, and take the covenant, you will undoubtedly choose to have him reinstated. Parsons has played the Harlequin one night for me; now, by this means, should sickness or any accident befall Yates or me you will be at a certainty; the entertainment need not be stopped, as he will then be ready." '

Hazlitt, who saw the 1820 revival in the middle of the Grimaldi era, wrote: 'It is called a speaking pantomime. We had rather it had said nothing. It is better to act folly than to talk it.' He could not, even in those changed times, be expected to foresee the pantomimes which were to follow!

At the time of the first production of *Harlequin's Invasion* Britain was at war with France and General Wolfe had just won, and died at, the Battle of Quebec. Garrick, fired with patriotic fervour, wrote a song for the pantomime, which was set to music by William Boyce, the theatre's director of music. It is still remembered and sung:

> 'Heart of oak are our ships,
> Heart of oak are our men,
> We always are ready,
> Steady, boys, steady!
> We'll fight and we'll conquer again and again.'

In making Harlequin speak, Garrick may have been influenced by the work of Goldoni, who was then at the height of his reforms of the *Commedia dell'Arte* in Italy, giving shape and style to the form.

After the death of Rich, in 1761, no significant new Harlequin appeared at Covent Garden. Woodward left the Lane to go into management in Dublin in 1758, but returned to London and Covent Garden four years later, and was there at the time of his death in 1777. He is always said to have been an 'Attitude Harlequin', basing his movements on the posture-master's poses to denote the emotion as distinct from Rich's mime. To the rhythm of the music he would perform a series of postures 'according to the vicissitudes demanded by the various passions represented'. To carry out the conventional routine of jumping through walls and windows a double was engaged. One night by some blunder the two Harlequins met in the centre of the stage, much to the amusement of the audience.

Garrick retired in 1776 and was succeeded by Sheridan, who continued the same policy for pantomime, even himself writing *Robinson Crusoe; or, Harlequin Friday*, produced in 1781; the date was January 29th, *after* the Christmas holiday!

[13]

For some time George Colman had been counselling the change from the classical or mythological Opening to a fairy tale or legend. It was he who, in September 1780, for his own Little Theatre, Haymarket, but now a Theatre Royal with a Summer Patent, wrote *The Genius of Nonsense*, 'an original, whimsical, operatical, pantomimical, farcical, electrical, naval, military, temporary Extravaganza'. 'The old fabulous history of Harlequin, Columbine, and Pantaloon', says the *Hibernian Magazine* of the following month, 'is the foundation on which this afterpiece is worked; and in the escapes, concealments, metamorphoses, and the *dénouement* differs very little from its numerous predecessors; but the wit, humour, and *temporary satire* with which the author has enlivened the whole, places it in an eminent degree above every competitor.'

W. J. Lawrence says:

'In the opening scene or prologue Harlequin is discovered sitting tailor fashion, and seriously contemplating suicide since it had become the *ton*. He determines upon stitching up his mouth, and is proceeding to put his purpose into execution, when his hand is stayed by the sudden appearance of the Genius of Nonsense, who remonstrates vigorously. Harlequin begs of her not to *break* the *thread* of his discourse, and explains that he is driven to desperation by the amount of nonsense put into his mouth at the winter theatres; subjoining the remark that if half the members of Parliament and a considerable number of other public men would only emulate his example, the world would be much the better for it. Then follows a lively conversation, in the course of which Harlequin gives it as his opinion that "formerly when his mummery was well contrived he had wit at his finger's end, and satire in every tumble, but that dullness and dialogue came in together." The Genius of Nonsense then introduces herself *in propria persona* to her parti-coloured servitor, who ejaculates in astonishment that he had always considered Genius and Nonsense irreconcilable terms. "Quite the contrary," is the quick reply; "it requires a great deal of genius to give nonsense spirit." The Genius then gives Harlequin an exhaustive account of all those whom she had taken under her particular care, laughs at his suicidal intention, and imperiously bids him participate once more in the joys of active life. Then follows the pantomime proper with a very notable caste. Handsome Jack Bannister, still in his teens, made an excellent, "Vocal and Rhetorical Harlequin," his dumb gymnastic counterpart being capably rendered by Philip Lamash. This was the time when the stupendous quack, Doctor Graham, was drawing all London to his "Temple of Health" in Pall Mall; and Colman with admirable forethought contrived to satirise this rare show in a scene painted in faithful verisimilitude by the facetious Ned Rooker, in the course of which Bannister *fils* took the house by storm with his imitation of the great dealer in rhodomontade. Rooker's scenery, by the way, must have been particularly fine, we are told by a contemporary that the view of the Camp in St. James's Park which concluded the performance, is perhaps as accurate and masterly a spectacle as ever appeared on the more extensive theatres of Covent Garden and Drury Lane.

'In proceeding to recite the following lines with a lavish interspersement of animal imitations, Harlequin made a clever point out of the admission, to another character, that his gifts were more rhetorical than vocal, and that, *unlike his father* (Charles) he had but an indifferent ear for music:

> "I'm Master of Forte-piano:
>   Notes suited to every case,
> Like puppies I yelp in Soprano,
>   Or growl, like a bull-dog in base.
> I can bark like a dog;
> I can grunt like a hog,
>   Squeak like pigs; or like asses can bray;
> Or turn'd to a fowl,
> I can hoot like an owl.
> Sure of all I'd be at,
> Can crow sharp, and quack flat;
>   Or gobble, like turkeys, all day."

'The humour of the introductory apology lay in the fact that Bannister *père*, the fine quality of whose vocal powers was beyond all dispute, was himself in the cast, and played the small part of Gammer Gurton. Gagging, tippling John Edwin, pre-eminent among low comedians, and the prince of burletta artists, likewise impersonated Dame Turton. It was played as an afterpiece to crowded houses until the end of the season, and never afterwards revived.'

The word extravaganza makes an early appearance in the author's description, and its meaning will become clearer in the next century.

It must have been obvious that pantomime was rapidly changing and giving a chance for the older playgoers to complain that it was not the same as it was in their youth, the recurring cry of every generation.

A TIME OF CHANGE

Before going on to the transitional era before the advent of Grimaldi and the ascendency of Clown at the turn of the century, there are one or two things to remember. As has been pointed out, though many pantomimes (often the new ones) were produced around Christmas, revivals were often staged at all times during the theatrical season at the Lane and the Garden, and during their closure at other theatres.

The pantomimes were mostly afterpieces of the double, or even triple, bills making up the long evenings favoured by playgoers of the day. One finds a Garrick or a Kemble playing classical rôles before the pantomime. The half-price system, which admitted a section of the audience at a reduced cost at a specified time during the evening, caused popular successes to be moved about the bill to allow a less affluent public to see this part of the performance.

When a new pantomime was produced at Christmas without half prices, with what to-day we would call a 'sitting duck' of an audience, it became a tradition to give the lower-class playgoers a moral lesson! George Lillo's 1731 play, *George Barnwell; or, The London Merchant*, was ideal with which to start the evening, with its lesson of how shame and degradation could come to one who did not obey his master. As early as 1749 *Barnwell* was being acted without a pantomime on Boxing Day. The following year it was joined by *The Beggar's Opera*, but in 1751 commenced its long association with pantomime (in this case *Harlequin Ranger*) which was to last well into the following century.

Eventually the play itself became a pantomime, *Harlequin George Barnwell; or, The London Prentice*, at Covent Garden in 1836. After that it is surprising to find it again played before the Drury Lane pantomime on Boxing Day 1854. What had been a custom had become a tradition, and when one becomes the other, as far as pantomime is concerned, it is hard to define!

The same must also be said of the playing of certain parts. It will have been noticed that at the Haymarket in 1780 both Charles Bannister and John Edwin played female parts: Bannister was Gammer Gurton and Edwin, Dame Turton. Bannister was also later, for a benefit, to play Polly in an *en travestie* production of *The Beggar's Opera*, also at the Haymarket in 1781. Thus it is no surprise to find Miss Abigle Antique in *The White Cat* played by William Chatterley in 1811 at the Lyceum, and the great Grimaldi, in an enveloping 'Big Head' appearing as Queen Rondabellona in *Harlequin and the Red Dwarf* in 1812 and as Dame Cecily Suet in *Harlequin Whittington* in 1814 at Covent Garden. Enter the pantomime Dame by custom or tradition?

Besides Colman and Sheridan, another writer, Charles Dibdin, was turning his attention to this entertainment and it was he who was before long to re-shape the whole face of pantomime. Before this finally happened the actor was virtually to take charge from the writer.

Carlo Delpini, who had played Pierrot at Drury Lane from 1776 under Garrick, shifted the emphasis from Harlequin to Pierrot; this character until now had been the blundering servant of Pantaloon or a country bumpkin in the traditional mould of what we know as the Clowns of the plays of Shakespeare and the Elizabethan dramatists. Delpini anglicized the character and gave him what has been called by Wilson Disher 'the stamp of the overgrown schoolboy which English audiences have always loved'.

Delpini was responsible for the 'dumb show' in Sheridan's *Robinson Crusoe; or, Harlequin Friday*. The pantomime ran for thirty-eight nights, a long first run in those days. Sheridan united once and for all the Opening with the Harlequinade. Whereas in some of the early pantomimes Harlequin and his companions had not even appeared in the Openings, Sheridan made Harlequin and Clown play parts in the story, which was told in two sections and was followed by a two-part Harlequinade.

Lawrence says:

'The scene shifters must have had a lively time of it, seeing that there were no fewer than eight changes in the first act alone! Some excellent scenery was provided by De Loutherbourg, who, under Garrick, had made many vital improvements in *mise en scène*. Sheridan was only directly responsible for the prelude, which opened with the scene in Crusoe's hut, and thenceforward adhered closely to the lines of Defoe's narrative. The harlequinade was arranged by Carlo Delpini, who played Crusoe in the opening. Guiseppe Grimaldi was Friday. According to *The Percy Anecdotes*, Sheridan on one occasion played the part of Harlequin Friday, through the unavoidable absence of Grimaldi. The comic scenes were rendered very amusing by means of a magic cask and an appropriation of the bibulous Friars from *The Duenna*; and a clever trick change from the exterior of a convent to that of a windmill, with the clown fastened to the revolving sails, came in for a large share of the nightly applause. Popular favour maintained the Drury Lane pantomime intermittently on the boards until Easter, 1816, when the great success at Covent Garden of Pocock's melo-drama on the same subject consigned it to limbo. Sheridan's production had been revived for a few nights at the same theatre, "by permission of the proprietors of Drury Lane," in the middle of July, 1813, when Joe Grimaldi played Crusoe and Young Bologna Friday. Its final appearance on the metropolitan stage was made at Sadler's Wells in 1814 on the occasion of Grimaldi's benefit. The performance was otherwise notable for the *début* of the immortal Joey's wayward son in the part of Friday. It will thus be seen that three generations of Grimaldis had entertained the public in this truly famous pantomime.'

Delpini was responsible for many other pantomimes and innovations, although his *Aladdin; or, The Wonderful Lamp*, at Covent Garden in 1788, was criticized for being more Harlequinade than Opening, though this had been written by John O'Keefe.

With Pierrot–Clown now in charge, Harlequin and the others receded into the background. Delpini even produced one pantomime without a Columbine in 1794, a version of the old ballad *Robin Hood; or, Merry Sherwood*.

It took a dancer, James Byrne, if not to restore Harlequin, at least to put him in the place and costume in which he was to remain for the rest of his days. Instead of the loose-fitting belted jacket and trousers of Rich and his successors he devised a costume that we would now describe as body tights, skin-fitting without a wrinkle with silk diamond-shaped patches of various colours sewn all over and outlined with tinsel and spangles. He added a white frilled collar and 'bicorn' hat, with a less cumbersome mask covering the head and part of the face.

Harlequin still carried his magic flat bat or wand, given to him by the Benevolent Agent, a symbol of potency. Its stubby handle often followed the *Commedia dell'Arte* tradition and was used as a phallic symbol. In fact even in later seemingly most innocent juvenile drama-sheets the bat handle appears to be a phallus, much as in the comedies of ancient Greece and Rome, an echo from the past, from where Harlequin and his fellows claim their descent.

ENTER JOSEPH GRIMALDI

Joseph Grimaldi came from a theatrical ancestry. His father Guiseppe Grimaldi arrived in London·from the fairs of Italy and France and after dancing at the King's Theatre became, in 1758, a member of Garrick's company at Drury Lane, making himself indispensable with Delpini in the production of the pantomimes and playing, in turn, most of its characters, for the next thirty years until he died in 1788.

During the summer, when the Lane was closed, Grimaldi often appeared at Sadler's Wells Theatre and it was here, in 1781, that he introduced his son, Joseph, to the public, a mere child of almost three years of age. The following year Joey was with his father at the Lane. He made a name for himself playing imps, gnomes, monkeys, cats, or in any utility parts necessary. After his father died he continued the association with the Wells and became 'Mister Grimaldi' on the bills before the century was over.

He was the Punch and Clown in *Harlequin's Amulet* at the Lane and just as Byrne changed Harlequin so Grimaldi, with the assistance of the writer Thomas Dibdin, and the actor, writer and producer Charles Farley, soon changed Clown into the central character it was to remain as long as the Harlequinade lasted.

Thomas Dibdin, the illegitimate son of Charles, started his career at Sadler's Wells, where he began to devise pantomimes, coming to Covent Garden in 1799. Charles Farley, an actor at the Garden from 1782, had played in pantomime there from his earliest days.

Dibdin and Farley made an ideal combination and had been working on a new idea for some years, with Joseph Grimaldi in mind, but, we are told, had not been able to persuade the management of Covent Garden to take notice:

'It was usual at Covent Garden to begin preparing for Christmas six or seven months before, but the customary signs were wanting in 1806, and Dibdin was much discomfited, when Thomas Harris, the manager, knocked at his door just six weeks before holiday time, and saluted him with: "Well, Dibdin, we cannot do without a pantomime from you after all!" Dibdin expostulated in vain, and at last proposed to produce one he had by him. "What!" exclaimed the manager, "that cursed *Mother Goose* you are so wedded to? Well, she has one recommendation, she has no finery about her;" and so it was settled. Now, the Covent Garden management had always been noted for sparing no expense in such matters, its liberality extending so far as to provide a good dinner at the Piazza Coffee-house on the first evening of the pantomime, and find a pint of wine apiece for the principal performers every night the pantomime was played. Now economy was the order of the day. Harris, confident of failure, would risk no more than he could help. Grand scenery and gorgeous dresses were forbidden; and had it not been for Grimaldi's intervention, Harlequin must have capered in an unspangled jacket. *Harlequin Mother Goose; or, The Golden Egg* was produced on 29 December; Simmons played Mother Goose; Pietro Bologna, Pantaloon; John Bologna (his son), Harlequin; Miss Searle, Columbine; while Grimaldi played Squire Bugle (afterwards Clown), it being his first appearance at Covent Garden in that character. To the astonishment of all concerned, the pantomime succeeded; the people crowded the house night after night, each audience seeming more enthusiastic than its predecessor; and when, on the eighty-eighth night of performance, Bologna and Grimaldi took their benefit, the receipts only wanted two shillings to make up six hundred and eighty pounds. A run of ninety-two nights brought the season to an end.'

It must be remembered that *Mother Goose* was naturally part of a double or triple bill, often performed with George Frederick Cooke in one of his famous Shakespearean rôles to start the evening, and concluding with a short ballet.

This pantomime, the fruit of Grimaldi's experience both at the Lane and the Wells, with the co-operation of the author and stage manager (as the director was then termed) set a pattern for pantomime for the next thirty years. Within the traditional structure was created a vehicle for comedy, spectacle and satire, even more rigid than it had been before. In the Opening the head and shoulders of the principal characters were covered and completely masked with 'Big Heads' which helped to conceal them before 'transformation' at the climax of the story. Grimaldi changed the costume and make up of Clown, creating his own individual style, one which, with little alteration, remained 'traditional' for the character.

An idea of the type of pantomime evolved will best be understood from the 'Argument' or plot of *Mother Goose* (a nursery-rhyme character of long standing):

'Avaro, the miserly guardian of Colinette, breaks a promise he had given Colin to allow him to marry his ward, in favour of Squire Bugle, a rich widower of repulsive manners, and as disagreeable to Colinette as Colin is the reverse. The piece opens with preparations for the Squire's marriage with Colinette, which are interrupted by the remonstrances of Colin. During the hubbub this occasions, the Beadle and Parish Constable bring Mother Goose before Squire Bugle as a reputed witch, and beg for her immediate punishment. Bugle condemns her to the ducking-stool, a sentence opposed by Colin, who espouses the cause of the old Dame, who, escaping from her persecutors, puts an end to the wedding festivities by raising the ghost of the Squire's first wife. Colin, however, cannot overcome Avaro's opposition, until Mother Goose presents him with her goose, famed for laying a golden egg every day, that he may offer it to Avaro, in exchange for his ward. The miser accepts the bird with rapture, but refuses to give up the damsel unless Colin consents to cutting it open, that he may satisfy his avarice at one swoop. Much against his conscience, Colin agrees to the sacrifice; but Mother Goose, appearing in the nick of time, saves her pet, and condemns Colin, Avaro, and the Squire to wear the shapes of Harlequin, Pantaloon, and Clown, and wander about the world contending for Colinette (transformed into Columbine), until the golden eggs, which she has cast into the sea, shall be recovered by one of them. The transformation takes place in the fifth scene, and the pursuit of the heroine is carried through fourteen scenes, until the relenting enchantress takes pity, and unites the lovers in her Submarine Pavilion.'

So much has been written about the genius of Joseph Grimaldi during his triumphs until his forced retirement in 1828 that it would need a complete book even to summarize his career! His business, his songs, 'Hot Codlins' and 'Tippity Witchet', were demanded again and again and became, just as did his name 'Joey', part and parcel of the Clown character. His own *Memoirs*, edited by Charles Dickens, were published in 1838, the year after he died. They have several times been reprinted, and were edited for a new edition in 1958 by his biographer, Richard Findlater, who had published *Grimaldi, King of Clowns* in 1955.

The whole panorama of Regency pantomime 1806–1836 was surveyed by David Mayer in 1969 in *Harlequin in His Element*.

It seems that Grimaldi's art, in a general survey of pantomime such as this, best speaks for itself in the pictures and their captions. For the first time pantomime is completely depicted in all its enchantment in the juvenile drama sheets, theatrical portraits, and tinsel pictures which began to make their appearance about the same time as Grimaldi rose to fame. These sheets of Characters, Scenes and Tricks, often embellished with full scenes showing the pantomimes in progress, give, as no words can, a perfect 'Penny Plain-Tuppence Coloured' picture of the period.

Grimaldi was also the subject for the brilliant pencil of Cruickshank and lesser copyists. These engravings have left behind a vivid impression of how he wove a spell over the masses, and one can see why pantomime more and more became a family entertainment, both at the Metropolitan and Minor theatres.

Grimaldi overworked and brought ill-health upon himself, not improved by a son, also Joseph, who, though given every opportunity, did not live up to his father's hopes, eventually being hurt in a drunken brawl and receiving injuries from which he never mentally recovered. In 1832, 'It was proved before the coroner that he died in a state of wild and furious madness.' A broken man, Grimaldi gave a memorable Farewell at Drury Lane in 1828 before he died in 1837.

This is not to say that there were not other Clowns and pantomime artists of great popularity appearing at the other theatres, but Grimaldi dominated the whole era.

In *Chambers's Journal* an anonymous author, writing in 1869, describes Grimaldi with what must have been a near contemporary eye;

'Acting and clowning have been dis-associated so long, that Grimaldi is almost beyond the comprehension of the present generation of playgoers. He was a great actor, who could extort tears in serious pantomime, and yet justify Kemble introducing him as the first low comedian in the country. Theodore Hook styled him the Garrick of clowns; and Harley called him the Jupiter of practical joke, the Michael Angelo of buffoonery, who, if he was grim all day, was sure to make folks chuckle at night. Joe never attempted any dangerous feats, and never padded in his life; he was no jumper, but a living embodiment of quiet fun. His pantomime was such that you could fancy he would have been the Pulcinello of the Italians, the Arlequin of the French—that he could have returned a smart repartee upon Carlin. His motions, eccentric as they were, were evidently not a mere lesson from the gymnasium; there was a will, a mind overflowing with, nay, living upon fun, real fun. Nobody ever saw a practical joke of Grimaldi's misfire. A common repeater of tricks might be out; but he who entered heart and soul into the mischief afloat, and enjoyed it as much as the youngest of his spectators, could never be at a loss. If he was, now and then, allowed to speak a word or two, they never came out as having been set down for him. Everybody thought they were the positive ebullitions of the wild frolic spirit which broke out of him. He was a master of grimace; and whether he was robbing a pieman, opening an oyster, affecting the polite, riding a giant cart-horse, imitating a sweep, grasping a red-hot poker, devouring a pudding, picking a pocket, beating a watchman, sneezing, snuffing, courting, or nursing a child, he was so extravagantly natural, that the most saturnine looker-on acknowledged his sway; and neither the wise, the proud, the fair, the young, nor the old were ashamed to laugh till tears coursed down their cheeks at Joe and his comicalities.

'Grimaldi went through work that would break the heart of a modern Clown, playing right through a pantomime of twenty scenes, and that at two theatres every evening. He would have scorned to share the honours with another.

'Grimaldi usually sang two songs in the course of a pantomime; his famous "Hot Codlins" being introduced to an appreciative world at Sadler's Wells, upon Easter Monday, 1819 and at this theatre on 17 March 1828 he made his last appearance before his final farewell at Drury Lane.'

It was Dibdin's *Mother Goose* that introduced pantomime to New York playgoers where it was seen, with an English Clown, Charles Parsloe, at the Bowery Theatre on Boxing Day 1831. It met with moderate success but pantomime failed to establish itself as firmly as in London. It was to have a short but brilliant revival with George L. Fox, said to be the greatest Clown since Grimaldi. His *Humpty Dumpty*, produced in 1868, held the stage till he went mad and died in 1877; with him pantomime also died in the States.

Though so far we have detailed the growth of pantomime in London, it must be remembered that up and down the country at the Theatres Royal the stock and circuit companies were producing their own versions, following London's lead. Most prominent actors, at one time or another, had to play Harlequin during their starring engagements. Edmund Kean at Exeter in 1813, before he came to Drury Lane, appeared after playing Faulkland in *The Rivals* as Harlequin in *The Corsican Fairy; or, Britannia's Triumph!*, a very topical Napoleonic pantomime, at the end of which the audience were regaled with: 'A superb view of the British Fleet in motion. In which Britannia rises out of the sea in Neptune's Car, drawn by sea horses'; an effect more easily realized at an Aquatic Theatre like Sadler's Wells than at a small country playhouse!

VICTORIAN FAIRYLAND, BURLESQUE AND EXTRAVAGANZA

After the era of Grimaldi, pantomime remained much the same, with many copyists or followers of the master. Principal among these was his pupil, Tom Matthews; often said to be the last of the traditional Clowns, he finalized the costume into the 'frilly' version which is used to this day, and accepted as the 'correct' Clown costume.

Social habits were changing fast in the 'thirties and 'forties. Railway expansion and easier travel created a vast new audience clamouring for entertainment, and a new morally-minded middle class emerged in reaction to the licentiousness of the Regency. The accession of Queen Victoria in 1837, and her marriage in 1840, began a vogue for family life and introduced Christmas as the children's festival subsequently hallowed by Dickens; even Prince Albert himself is credited with the introduction of the Christmas tree!

All this helped to foster a new fantastical fairy story with fairy queen and demon, a romantic pantomime exclusively for children at Christmas. There grew up a number of more sophisticated writers who catered for an adult audience both at Christmas and Easter; they created the burlesque or extravaganza, so often confused with pantomime, only because they often shared the same basic fairy tales or legendary subjects.

To take burlesque first, there has been a long tradition of burlesque and travesty in the British theatre, from *The Rehearsal* through *Tom Thumb* to *The Critic*, becoming in the mid-nineteenth century a flourishing genre. Plays, operas, classical legends and fairy stories were all treated irreverently, modern topical interpretations placed on old subjects and contemporary plays travestied. They and French *opéra bouffe* became, by the 'sixties and 'seventies, the target for the purity campaigners. The actresses played boys, scantily clad, the men played ladies, vulgarly as it was thought, which all tended to give burlesque a bohemian name.

Even in 1846 *Cruickshank's Comic Almanac* complained:
'The progress of burlesque at various theatres has done much to injure pantomimes, and it is feared the race of clowns will become extinct unless in these days of educational enlightenment some means are taken to train up fresh ones as the old ones drop off.'

In December 1855, at the Adelphi, Benjamin Webster produced *Jack and the Beanstalk; or, Harlequin and Mother Goose at Home Again*. It was called 'A grand coalition of Burlesque and Comic Pantomime for young and old'. Madame Celeste was Jack and Miss Wyndham Mother Goose. They became Harlequin and Columbine in the transformation *à la Watteau*, which contrasted pantomime ancient and modern and, incidentally, made Celeste a strong candidate for the title of the first Principal Boy.

The experiment was followed the next year with *Mother Shipton, her Wager; or, Harlequin Knight of Love, and The Magic Whistle*. Celeste was Sir Beau and Miss Wyndham Constance, before their transformation. *The Illustrated London News's* critic was optimistic in his statement that the new style was now universal:

'This theatre deservedly takes credit to itself for having originated the composite entertainment of burlesque-pantomime now generally adopted in preference to pantomime pure and simple. As public taste improves, public amusements aim at a higher and yet higher mark; and Christmas pieces are projected upon a scale of literary expense as well as scenic splendour little thought of in ruder periods.'

He must have been a devotee of burlesque, which went its own way and did not fully infiltrate into real pantomime for some time.

The authors of burlesques were some of the most brilliant wits and playwrights of their day. J. R. Planché, Gilbert à Beckett, the Brough Brothers, H. J. Byron, W. S. Gilbert, Robert Reece and F. C. Burnand spanned the era. Their stories, told in cleverly rhymed couplets peppered with brilliant puns and interspersed with new lyrics adapted to popular songs and excerpts from opera, found a public which filled the Olympic and the Lyceum under Madame Vestris and Charles Mathews, the Haymarket under Buckstone, the Gaiety under Hollingshead and the Royal Strand under the Swanboroughs.

The greatest confusion arises when these playwrights have taken a story which had been, or was later to become, the subject of a pantomime as the framework for a burlesque, and often one finds that many now popular pantomime stories were burlesques before they were ever to become Christmas entertainments.

In some cases too, characters now accepted as part and parcel of pantomime derive from burlesque. Widow Twankey made her first appearance in *Aladdin; or, The Wonderful Scamp* by H. J. Byron, who *invented* her and Pekoe, the Grand Vizier, for a burlesque at the Royal Strand in April 1861; both parts were played *en travestie*, as was Aladdin.

Byron also wrote *Cinderella; or, The Lover, The Lackey and The Little Glass Slipper*, 'a Fairy Burlesque Extravaganza', in 1860, in which Dandini and Buttoni appeared. Dandini derived his name from the valet in *La Cenerentola*, the opera by Rossini, to a libretto by Feretti, produced in Rome in 1817 and in London in 1820, and to the Dandy Lover, the fop or the over-dressed unsuccessful suitor for Columbine in the Grimaldi-era Harlequinades. The character still survives as Prince Charming's valet, over-dressed when disguised as his master, and apeing his manners. Buttoni, the Page, was to be anglicized as Buttons when *Cinderella* became a true pantomime. An excellent and informative history of this subject by W. Davenport Adams, *A Book of Burlesque*, was published in 1891.

These examples could be extended at great length, but this *must* be made clear, that burlesques were *not* pantomimes. They were very adult entertainments, by the standard of their day, and produced arbitrarily at any time of the year. It did become the custom to add these and extravaganzas to the general Christmas festivities, and they were sometimes presented at Easter when they became known as 'Easter Pieces'.

It is these entertainments that have been revived at the Players' Theatre, often heavily and cleverly revised to make them, as they were originally, topical, but unfortunately called pantomimes by the press and public, which has confused the younger and unwary historian. In fact the newly formed British Pantomime Association and its founder, Gyles Brandreth, have published as their first contribution to its 'preservation' two scripts, both of which are Strand Theatre burlesques by H. J. Byron, the *Cinderella* of 1860 and the *Aladdin* of 1861.

It is fairly safe to say that unless the name 'Harlequin' is included in the title, anything before the 'seventies was *not* intended or *produced* as a pantomime.

If only reference was made to the playwright's *own description* of his work on the script, playbill or programme, all would be clear. This applies to every form of dramatic work; except for very rare cases, the author knows and states what he intended! An infallible rule which, if followed, would prevent many foolish mistakes.

To add to the so-called confusion many of the burlesque playwrights of the day also wrote pantomimes and extravaganzas; but if one takes the listed works from Allardyce Nicoll of only three of the most famous authors of the period one finds Planché credited with but four pantomimes against twenty-five burlesques and extravaganzas, similarly Byron with eight against sixty-three, but on the opposite side Blanchard with sixty-five pantomimes and only nine of the other class. Gilbert wrote only one pantomime but numerous burlesques, etc. If there was *no* misunderstanding in Victorian days why should there be now?

Extravaganza is described by Grove as:

'Any work of art in which accepted forms are caricatured, and recognised laws violated, with a purpose.'

This could easily cover pantomime and in fact the name extravaganza did appear in a description in 1780, but generally its use in Victorian times was for anything which could not be legitimately fitted into the category of burlesque and was not pantomime, as well as the new form of entertainment, revue, which made its appearance under the wing of Planché in 1825. He had experimented with the idea on and off for thirty years without transplanting this French entertainment on to English soil, but the seed though sown had to wait many years to grow successfully; meantime a 'go as you please' entertainment sheltered under the name of extravaganza.

Also during the early and mid-Victorian years music hall grew from a public house entertainment in the 'forties (the first use of the name in this sense is at the Surrey Music Hall in 1848), and by the 'seventies was a flourishing part of the entertainment world in what their managers called Palaces of Variety.

Having cleared, one hopes once and for all, the pantomime stage of both burlesque and extravaganza, the fairy-land that was set out before the Victorian child at Christmas can be fully appreciated and understood.

The theatres were finally liberated from the monopoly of the Patent Houses in 1843, which allowed for the growth of many large suburban theatres, as well as the expansion of the existing Minor theatres. Some of the Saloon theatres, which were on the borderline between music hall and theatre, took the opportunity to become legitimate theatres; ones like the Britannia, Hoxton and the Grecian, City Road, became at once the established homes of spectacular drama and pantomime. Every district round London vied with each other to give its local audience something special at Christmas. The music halls, still only operating under a Singing and Dancing Licence, could not compete or give any full dramatic entertainment; they did not achieve their freedom and come under the Lord Chamberlain's jurisdiction until 1911.

Although the mime and dumb show was not necessarily in the scripts which were submitted to the Lord Chamberlain's office, the *Illustrated London News* reported in 1851, '[it] placed some restrictions on the pantomimes, and required the comic portions to be submitted to official investigation as well as the introductory dialogue. The difficulties of this regulation, however, have been surmounted, and this class of pieces is still as amusing and the present year more expensively got up than ever.'

This kind of trouble with censorship was often to recur over invented 'gags', mostly impromptu at first and then retained, which had not been approved by the Lord Chamberlain, placing the manager of the theatre at the mercy of the common informer.

Every actor-manager had to produce a pantomime at Christmas. Charles Kean, at the Princess's, was as famous for his work in this field as for his lavish Shakespearean revivals. Benjamin Webster at the Adelphi, Samuel Phelps at the Wells, were also as much involved as were the names which have lived mainly for their association with pantomime, like the Conquests at the Grecian and the Surrey, while amphitheatres like Astley's staged Equestrian pantomimes. Pantomime became firmly established up and down the country, but it was the rivalry between Drury Lane and Covent Garden (even after it became a sedate Opera House) which set the pattern for production, and for writers like E. L. Blanchard, who wrote sixty-five pantomimes between 1844 and 1888, often for both houses the same year! His work spans the old style and the new which came into being at the end of the 'seventies.

The fertile imagination of the Victorian authors invented magic fairy stories with appeal to the romantic mid-Victorian family; as yet the now familiar plots and titles did not dominate pantomime. Titles got longer and longer just as the daily playbills got larger and larger. Those of the Adelphi in mid-century reached 20″ by 30″, the size now of a double crown poster! They must have been difficult to handle, even more so when the heavy black ink on the thin paper was hardly dry from the morning's printing. One reads of the ladies' complaints of ruined gloves! The large playbills were needed to accommodate the long titles and often the long-winded humorous description of scenes and characters, as well as other information of the evening's entertainment. The pantomime at the Adelphi for Christmas 1845 was called, *Harlequin and POONOOWINGKEEWANGFLIBEEDEEFLOBEEDEEBUSKEEBANG; or, The King of the Cannibal Islands*. The Opening covered seven scenes and the Harlequinade had seventeen changes, finishing up in 'The Hall of Christmas'.

The evening had started at seven with an adaptation of Dickens' *Cricket on the Hearth*, followed by a one-act farce *The Phantom Breakfast*, even before the pantomime, which must have gone on till nearly midnight!

The whole pantomime industry, as it became, employed many people for the best part of the year. After the writing, scenic and costume preparations, the work of engaging the company began. Towards Christmas the auditions for children became a useful publicity-story for the illustrated journals. In 1867, accompanying a picture of the scene at Drury Lane stage door (Picture 91), a reporter said:

'A month or two before Christmas the managers of each theatre, or those whom they depute to select the required number of juvenile "supers" for the intended performance, are wont to receive many more applications for this kind of employment than they can possibly grant. Certain days and hours must of course be appointed for the settlement of this business, which is but one part, and not the most urgent or difficult, of the vast and multifarious arrangements needful to the production of a new pantomime or extravaganza. Any curious observer of the ways of social life happening to stand under the colonnade of Drury Lane Theatre on such an occasion might have seen what the pencil of our own Artist has delineated in the Engraving on another page. The big boys, irrepressible in their mirthful excitement, capering or turning heels-over-head, or rudely thrusting themselves forward, to claim the doorkeeper's attention; the smaller boys nearly lost in the tumult, or timidly standing at their mother's side; the girls, some almost grown to be women, and having a bold or pert look on their faces which it is sad to see; others who still keep the charm of innocent childhood, which may, even on the boards of a theatre, be preserved from the taint of vice, if the parent's example and teaching have been good; the idle bystanders looking on, with characteristic jeers and comments; the steady policeman who maintains peace, if not quiet and order, among the jostling mob of candidates for theatrical engagements, whose shrill voices raise a fresh clamour whenever the door is opened;—these are the human materials of the *mise en scène*. Let us hope that the poor children will by-and-by find some more substantial industry and some more useful instruction than they are likely to get in Drury Lane; but we have no right to find fault with their present quest of employment in the meantime. They might too easily be doing worse. Who will give them a chance of doing better?'

The following year the same magazine took its readers inside a theatre, visiting a rehearsal of *Humpty Dumpty and Dame Trot and her Cat; or, The Old Woman from Babyland and the Little Bachelor who Lived by Himself* at the Lyceum (picture 92):

'We are inclined to hold with those who never want to know how a puzzle that amuses them is done. We think that any bit of parlour magic or other cleverness is best unexplained. We are never for shaking the bran out of dolls; but an artist has furnished us with an interesting sketch of what may be called the disenchanting sort, and we are but accomplices with him in appending a few words. He shows a bit of the inner life of the stage, the drilling of the youths and maidens who contribute so largely to the fun and the grace of the spectacles which are now in full swing. The process is one which requires patience and painstaking, especially with the masculine recruits, girls always learning everything much more quickly than the stupider sex. It may be mentioned, also, that as the remuneration given to this class of artist is not very large, it is naturally supplied from a not very cultivated portion of the population. Which things being considered, it is rather surprising how well the stage business is learned, and how effective are the complicated combinations of groups, how rapid the manoeuvres, and how steady the phalanx. All this is due to the laborious training and practice which the Illustration depicts. Boy by boy has to be vigilantly watched, and it has to be made perfectly clear to his possibly not over-lucid mind exactly what he is to do, where he is to stand, and when he is to distinguish himself, or a single blunder might throw the whole corps into confusion and destroy the picturesque effect contemplated by the ballet master. He has also to be taught presence of mind, and to know that if the clown or pantaloon is seized with an unusual access of vigour and happens to knock him about a little, he is not to be frightened, or to howl, as his instinct might prompt, far less is he to try to get out of the way. With some of the smallest performers (whose feats one witnesses with a certain regret, for a hot theatre at midnight is not the place for infants), these things have to be taught with kindness and playfulness, or the little things will break down; with the bigger ones, a certain peremptoriness, to say the least of it, is found efficacious. There is not much trouble with the young ladies, save in exceptional cases. They like the work, they are made to look as pretty as possible, and they know that they will be admired, more or less; their instructor has, therefore, a comparatively easy and pleasant task. But, in any case, the drill is frequent and severe; and the audiences who applaud the gaily dressed and adroit creatures who perform before them know little how many hours of labour and practice are represented by a scene or a dance, and do not know that the artists have most likely walked long distances to rehearsals, probably in bad weather, and that, after protracted exercise, they have to walk home again, weary and hungry, and seldom to any very luxurious meal. We would not spoil anybody's pleasure, but there is no harm in letting people recollect that there is a large and an industrious class which earns its living by very hard work, performed to give the richer among us a pleasant evening.'

Something of the year-long backstage preparations can be gathered from *The Illustrated Sporting and Dramatic News* in December 1874, where the following accompanied the illustration (picture 99):

'Being a privileged person, I pass through the stage door unquestioned, along a short corridor on to the stage; then, turning to the left, walk by long avenues of dust-begrimed scenery, where almost shrouded in darkness stand wings of old castles, pennants of palaces, and once brilliant sunsets, all looking dark and grim in the half light. Diving down one of these dark lanes, I come to a flight of old and rickety stairs, where, on ascending and passing at the top through a swing-door, is the open Sesame to the Bluebeard chamber of pantomime mystery, a long low room with skylights. In every nook and cranny and hanging from the roof are stage properties—birds, beasts, and fishes, from the roaring lion to the lowly porker; and in remote corners, where the light in half pity seems hesitating to penetrate, lie the heads of kings, nobles, and plebeians, some cut off in their prime (through exhausted exchequers), others in the last stage of decay (worn out by success), but all, begrimed and dusty, ignominiously heaped up together—princes, their vassals and minions, and favourite animals sharing alike one grave, showing that even in the pantomime of life we must all come to one common lot. Standing against the walls, and suspended from the beams that support the roof, are implements of the chase, weapons of offence and defence, family plate, small articles of furniture, and even the remains of a last sumptuous banquet may be seen littering the shelves and pigeon-holes of the walls. And still in the hour of their humility and degradation the conscience of these many heartless princes and moated castle barons may be pricked by the weapons they have used in stage torture and bloody crimes, shelved before their staring and bloodshot eyes. Avaunt! no more of these paper ghosts of long forgotten pantomimes. We no more tremble at their misdeeds. Let us turn to their creators, who are now busily engaged in building up fresh images of distortion, making the thousand things for the production of the forthcoming pantomime. There are four other rooms; one is the sanctum of the property master, where the designs are sketched; in the other three rooms these designs are carried out, one for carpentry, another for manufacturing jewellery and *bric à brac* to adorn the transformation and palatial scenes. In one of the rooms are women engaged in cutting out and making up the drapery for the properties.

'Passing through the carpenters' shop and along a short passage, we enter the *atelier* of scenic art—a very long lofty room, one of the largest of the kind in Great Britain. Here occasionally the author of the beautiful and artistic scenes which have embellished so many plays brought out under the energetic manager, Mr. F. B. Chatterton, may be seen employed in designing the most important scenes, and fitting them into the exact miniature of the stage (an indispensable article in good paint rooms). In other parts of the studio assistant artists are carrying out the designs, others cutting down trees, building up castles, and wiping out sunsets; some mixing colours, boiling size, &c. Leaving these in their laborious efforts to please the British public, we pass by one side of the flies, and on turning down a long corridor with dressing-rooms to right and left enter a neatly furnished room lighted by a skylight. A cheerful fire in the grate has the usual tom-cat asleep before its screen. Sitting round a table in the centre of the apartment are ladies unpicking robes which have adorned many a lovely princess of departed dynasties, and making them up with fresh silks and satins, ready to drape the fair forms of daughters of the reigning monarch of pantomime.'

The magic that was set before the wondering eyes of the children, and the bustle backstage seen from the wings (pictures 93 and 95) before the tired but happy return to suburbia (picture 94), have been caught by the contemporary artists, who also were often at pains to show how it was worked.

The *Illustrated Sporting and Dramatic News*, 1874, shows the equipment under the stage of the Princess's Theatre, 'The Star Trap' (picture 96), and gives the following description:

'The ingenious piece of mechanism by which, in pantomime, extravaganza and what may be called diabolical drama, "sprites" or "imps" are shot through the floor of the stage, is called the "Star Trap". It is well worth a visit below the stage to see the charging of the curious catapult, and the rapid flight of the human missile. In the scene represented by our artist a lady of the ballet is leaning against the frame of a large windlass, and near to her an old "dresser". In an open space stands the machinery of the trap. It is composed of an open square wooden frame in which a platform works up and down by means of very heavy counterweights. Of course, when no force is used to bring the platform down, the counterweights raise it to the top of the frame, which is directly beneath the opening of the trap in the floor of the stage. The trap itself is of a circular form, and is composed of sixteen sections of inch and a half planking, which are so lightly secured to the surrounding flooring that the least pressure from beneath forces them open. The trap is not visible in our illustration, as the platform, which works in the frame, is brought by the counterweights close against it. The clown has just descended. A carpenter, too, is holding a piece of cord, which comes from the stage above, where it is held by the stage manager. The cord is suddenly pulled, the carpenter holding it cries "Prepare", and certain men who are lounging about rush forward and seize hold of the platform beneath the trap. The cord is pulled a second time, and the word is "Unshore Trap". The platform is brought down, but it requires all the men's strength to do it, although others assist them by raising the counterweights. The clown steps forward and takes his stand on the platform in the frame. The cord is now pulled for the third time! The cry is "Send up". The men quit their hold of platform and weights, and Mr Sausage and Cat Stealer is shot through the open trap on to the stage above.'

Percy Fitzgerald, in a book which is a mine of useful information, under the title of *The World Behind the Scenes*, published in 1881, adds to the general picture:

'All will recall in some elaborate transformation scene how quietly and gradually it is evolved. First the "gauzes" lift slowly one behind the other— perhaps the most pleasing of all scenic effects—giving glimpses of "the Realms of Bliss," seen beyond in a tantalising fashion. Then is revealed a kind of half-glorified country, clouds and banks, evidently concealing much. Always a sort of pathetic and at the same time exultant strain rises, and is repeated as the changes go on. Now we hear the faint tinkle—signal to those aloft on "bridges" to open more glories. Now some of the banks begin to part slowly, showing realms of light, with a few divine beings—fairies—rising slowly here and there. More breaks beyond and fairies rising, with a pyramid of these ladies beginning to mount slowly in the centre. Thus it goes on, the lights streaming on full, in every colour and from every quarter, in the richest effulgence. In some of the more daring efforts, the *femmes suspendues* seem to float in the air or rest on the frail support of sprays or branches of trees. While, finally, perhaps, at the back of all, the most glorious paradise of all will open, revealing the pure empyrean itself, and some fair spirit aloft in a cloud among the stars, the apex of all. Then all motion ceases; the work is complete; the fumes of crimson, green, and blue fire begin to rise at the wings; the music bursts into a crash of exultation; and, possibly to the general disenchantment, a burly man in a black frock steps out from the side and bows awkwardly. Then to shrill whistle the first scene of the harlequinade closes in, and shuts out the brilliant vision. Some of the more ambitious of these transformation scenes, notably those of Covent Garden, are remarkable works for the daring spirit in which they are conceived and their genuine magnificence. The variety of resources brought into play, the bold use made of the opportunities offered on so fine a stage, the enormous quantity of auxiliaries to be marshalled, the variety of design presented year after year, are significant of English energy, and cannot be approached in foreign theatres.

'The ingenuity exhibited in the aerial displays—girls apparently floating in the air at great heights—has to be supplemented by extraordinary precautions to prevent accidents. These "irons," as they are called, to which the performers are strapped, are made of the finest, best-tempered metal, and their shape must be ingeniously contrived to supply strength in company with the artistic requirements. This element is generally secured by extending them below the stage in the shape of long levers, which take their share of the weight. But large platforms, or *équipements*, as the French call them, are the essential portions of every "Transformation," consisting of a vast stage rising slowly from below, and suspended by ropes and counterpoises, and so nicely balanced that a couple of carpenters can raise them, although burdened by a score of *figurantes*, each strapped to her iron. This is the principle which underlies all these effects, but it is infinitely varied, and there are even platforms upon platforms, which rise in their turn after the first has arisen. Thus allusion has been made to the "crowning of the edifice" at the close of the transformation, when, perhaps, a semicircular group of fairies will rise, and from out this group a central figure will mount slowly, becoming the apex, as it were, of the whole. Then it will be noted that the semicircle begins to open, the group to separate, and the figures to glide down and forward by some mysterious agency. It is contrived by ingenious machinery, called by the French *parallèle*. This consists of a number of light pedestals, about twelve feet in height, which are ranged closely around a centre pedestal, the tops being drawn close to it by cords brought down and secured to a windlass worked by a man who ascends with the machine. At the proper moment he "lets go", and the weight of the figures, checked by counterpoises, allows the pedestals to open out, exactly as the ribs of an umbrella would do. The whole machine is complete in itself, and is kept "in stock," as it were, and can be fitted to many varieties of effect.

'We are so accustomed to what are called "transformation scenes," and so familiar with the various devices, that few consider that it is quite a modern innovation. Mr. Beverley may be said to be the inventor of those unfolding and slowly developing effects to which it is now found almost impossible to impart any novel effect. On Boxing-night 1849, Planché produced the *Island of Jewels* at the Lyceum under the Vestris management. He says: "The novel and yet exceedingly simple falling of the leaves of a palm tree which discovered six fairies supporting a coronet of jewels, produced such an effect as I scarcely remember having witnessed on any similar occasion up to that period. Year after year Mr. Beverley's powers were taxed to outdo his former outdoings. The last scene became the *first* in the estimation of the management. The most complicated machinery, the most costly materials, were annually put in requisition. As to me, I *was positively painted* out. Dutch metal in the ascendant. Mr. C. Mathews once informed me that he had paid between £60 and £70 for gold tissue for the dresses of the supernumeraries in the last scene of a burlesque." It is curious to read these naïve complaints written in 1872, not long after writing which one of his old burlesques was revived at some theatre, and the practical stage manager, seeing that the delicate wit and fine allusions would go over the heads of the audience, chopped and hewed at the piece, putting in business and cutting out talk lines, until the old writer almost shed tears of rage and vexation.'

The 'sixties saw the climax of Victorian pantomime in the Grimaldi tradition. Times were changing rapidly, the world of the theatre outside was invading the realm of Harlequin and Clown. Burlesque, *opèra bouffe* and the music halls were beginning to undermine the tradition like some fifth column! A few random examples point the way things were going in the decade.

'Harlequin' was dropped from the title at Covent Garden in 1868 for *Robinson Crusoe; or, Friday and the Fairy*, but returned on and off. At Drury Lane it was still *de rigeur* till 1879, then dropped for *Blue Beard*, but made odd appearances there as late as 1888. It lingered on out of London for some time yet.

The principal characters appeared without 'Big Heads', which were reserved for processions and crowds. As the Harlequinade shrank so the Opening grew, there became less and less connection between them and two distinct companies were engaged. By the end of the century the transformation had lost its real meaning and was the finale of part one, where a Fairy Queen gave her hero a Vision or a Dream of Fairyland, the Land of Toys, or some such delight, usually an opportunity for a ballet on a large scale. The second half of the nineteenth century saw a rebirth of ballet at the Alhambra and the Empire, where some of the traditions of the romantic era were kept alive after they had been dropped by the opera houses. Ballets in pantomime rose to new spectacular heights as time went on, employing the leading ballerinas of the day.

Costumes too secured the attention of well-known designers. Alfred Chasemore, Alfred Thompson, Wilhelm, Alias and Comelli were to span the era with brilliant invention.

Gradually stories drawn from *The Arabian Nights*, Perrault, Grimm, Hans Andersen and nursery legend became the stock in trade of the pantomime writer, but in the end only a handful of subjects were left in general use.

Popular songs from other fields were being introduced. W. B. Fair, a music hall singer, famous for his song 'Tommy make room for your Uncle', which became a catch-phrase in its day, sang a version, 'Sally make room for your Uncle', at Covent Garden in *Cinderella* in 1873.

Actors who had made their names in pantomime were now taking music hall engagements at other times of the year; J. H. Macdermott, who had been well known at Covent Garden before he introduced the word 'Jingo' to the language at the Pavilion in 1877, and James Fawn, an actor turned comedian, were among them.

The casting of the main parts was also undergoing a change, due this time mainly to the influence of burlesque. As has been noted, the idea of a burlesque-pantomime was tried at the Adelphi with Madame Celeste as a Principal Boy—Harlequin in *Jack and the Beanstalk; or, Harlequin and Mother Goose at Home Again* in 1855, which makes her the first of a long line of beanstalk-climbers. It was some time before real pantomime capitulated; *Cinderella* at Covent Garden, 1864, had a male Prince and Valet but female Sisters. In 1875 at Drury Lane both Prince and Dandini were girls and the Sisters men. *Aladdin* at Covent Garden in 1865 was a girl (Rachel Sanger), so was Abdulla in *Ali Baba* in 1866. Peter Piper at the Lyceum in 1868 was a girl (Caroline Parks). At Drury Lane

Prince Felix in *Jack in the Box* in 1873 was a girl (Harriet Coveny), so was Walter Truelove, the hero of *Children in the Wood* at the Adelphi in 1874. When the Babes in the Wood story became linked with the Robin Hood legend at Drury Lane in 1880 both the hero and all his merry men were female!

The theatre has had a long tradition of *travestie* from the days of the Restoration playwrights. Peg Woffington as a female volunteer in male attire in 1746 recited an epilogue 'in an attempt to make our men stand', as well as appearing in the famous 'breeches parts'. Eliza Vestris later swept the town in Moncrieff's *Giovanni in London* in 1817 and as Macheath in 1820, though she was not the first female highwayman by any means. Vestris continued to play boys in the burlettas and extravaganzas written for her by Planché, as did many of her lesser contemporaries. In opera there were many opportunities, both intended or usurped, for male impersonation. In *Aladdin; or, His Wonderful Lamp*, a melodramatic romance by Charles Farley, Mrs Charles Kemble (Theresa De Camp) played the title rôle at Covent Garden in 1813. Grimaldi appeared as Kasrac, a dumb slave, in this Easter entertainment. This led Farley to some experiments in pantomime. In 1815, at Covent Garden, in *Harlequin and Fortunio*, he had a female character in the Opening masquerading as a man, but unmasked and discovered before being transformed into Columbine. In 1819 at Drury Lane, in *Jack and the Beanstalk; or, Harlequin and the Ogre*, Jack, in the Opening, was played by Eliza Povey, but when transformed into Harlequin, Bologna was substituted.

Three pantomimes, written by Charles Farley for Elizabeth Poole in the post-Grimaldi era at Covent Garden, are of interest: *Hop o' my Thumb and his Brothers; or, Harlequin and the Ogre*, 1831; *Puss in Boots; or, Harlequin and the Miller's Son*, 1832; and *Old Mother Hubbard and her Dog; or, Harlequin and the Tales of the Nursery*, 1838. In all of these she played young boys, Hop o' my Thumb, Josselyn and Cupid, exploiting her childish charm and voice, but not taking part in the Harlequinade.

Though these are early principal boys they are as yet only children's parts, not the fully mature characters they were to become in the 'sixties and 'seventies after a stint in burlesque! But before this, 'Women's Lib' had temporarily taken over Harlequin when Madame Celeste played the character *à la Watteau* in 1855. In reverse it was remarked as 'a Novelty' in 1911 when Millie Doris played Widow Twankey at Birmingham.

At the less progressive theatres around London and in the provinces the old order did not change so quickly, but double Harlequinade characters bolstered up the fun and a female Harlequin called Harlequina was invented. The 'traditional' theatres, like the Britannia and the Grecian, tended to rely on invention both of stories and weird and wonderful characters. At the Britannia Sara Lane held sway with the Lupino family.

It became traditional for the Clown and his fellows to be 'foreign' and belong to families with long pantomime tradition, like the Grimaldis, the Bolognas, the Martinettis, the Lauris, but among these English families grew up: the Paynes, the Vokes, the Conquests and many more.

The Conquests, an inspired *nom du thèâtre* for a family whose real name was Oliver, made pantomime animals of every kind synonymous with the name for three generations, at the Grecian, the Surrey and the Lane.

The name Lupino or Luppino is to be found among scene painters, dancers and pantomimists in the 18th and early 19th centuries, a respected Anglo-Italian family whose ancestry could be traced back for many years. The name was 'adopted' by George Hook (1820–1902), who at one time had been in partnership with a genuine 'Italian' Luppino, calling themselves 'The Luppinis'. After a split and change of partners Hook retained the name, as 'Lupino'. Not only did his family and their descendants adopt the name but later their historian unfortunately added the *original* ancestry to *their* family tree and created chaos in every branch of pantomimia!

George Hook Lupino had many children, including George Junr, who became Clown at the Britannia, while some married into the Lane family. The self-styled Lupinos added a brilliant chapter to traditional pantomime through Stanley, Barry and Lupino Lane and his son Lauri, keeping alive the trap work, acrobatics and all that the old Harlequinade really meant.

The ladies from *opéra bouffe* and the halls began to appear in pantomime. Among them was Nellie Power ('The boy I love is up in the gallery' and 'La di da' were two of her songs), whose male impersonations made her an ideal choice for Principal Boy; she was at Covent Garden in 1875 as the Prince in *Cinderella*.

Augustus Harris, Senior, presented pantomime at the Garden from 1871 till his death in 1873; his first pantomime, *Blue Beard*, incidentally, had a male Sister Ann. It was his son, also Augustus (nicknamed Druriolanus and Gusarris), who took over Drury Lane from Chatterton in 1879. Covent Garden more or less dropped out of the pantomime scene; only two more were staged in 1880 and 1881, then circus took over at Christmas for a few years. (except for 1888).

At the Lane the Vokes family had been in charge of pantomime, monopolizing all the principal parts, under Chatterton, from 1869 (except for 1873) until 1879–80. Fred, Jessie, Rosina and Walter Fawdon (who changed his name to Vokes) were a talented family, born and bred in the theatre, all singers, dancers and acrobats in the true tradition. Blanchard continued to write the pantomimes and the Vokeses seem to have fitted their 'routines' with little variation year after year to whatever story was chosen.

The Times in 1875 said:

'Who insists on criticism in a pantomime, and when the Vokes family are in that pantomime, who wants it? Drury Lane at Christmas time may be said for some years past to have represented the apotheosis of these clever people. Their astonishing, but always graceful antics would counterbalance far larger sins in the way of acting and singing than they commit.'

Later, in 1878, the *Daily Telegraph* reported:

'the Vokeses who, sublimely indifferent as to whether the story of Cinderella be a Sanskrit myth or a Greek fable, bring it to the level of contemporary intelligence by the exhibition of a consummately able "kicking up behind and before."

'These wondrous Vokeses surpassed themselves last night. They brought the house down, metaphorically speaking, over and over again; the only wonder is that, physically speaking, they did not bring the wings and sky borders and the very planks of the stage itself down into the bargain. Impulsive Mr. Fred Vokes as the Baron Pumperknickl von Grogswig, accompanied by Mr. Fawdon Vokes as Kobold, his trusty servant, disdained to be shackled by the preliminary dreariness of an incantation scene in which some tiresome magician relates a prosy prologue for the edification of a number of supernumeraries in monstrous masks.

'Scarcely had the curtain risen and a number of children disguised as wild boars begun to disport themselves in a mountain pass and a woody glade in the Black Forest than Mr. Fred Vokes, attended by his *fidus Achates*, Mr. Fawdon Vokes, plunged like Homer *in medias res*, skipped on to the stage, and both began to throw their arms and legs about in the most wonderful manner.'

But they were rather wearing out their welcome. Another critic commented:

'They gave us a good deal of the old *pas de Vokes*. They dance exactly as they have danced for years past, and they do not even take kindly to the new tunes and choruses of the day so liberally suggested in Mr. Blanchard's book. If they want to retain their hold upon the public they should get someone to concoct for them new modes in which to display their exceptional powers.'

And in 1879 the *Daily Telegraph* said:

'Through attempting to do too much the Vokes family eventually succeeded in provoking a feeling of depression. There was no relief, no change, and never a charm of contrast, and everyone felt that the comic efforts of the brothers and sisters had been unduly and unnecessarily strained. For example, a ballet when properly dressed and cleverly danced is obviously intended to be looked at and admired. If there is any meaning in such a dance it should concentrate the attention of all present with the skill and grace and movement of the dancers. But that is impossible if at the same time the brothers and sisters Vokes are tumbling over cushions, indulging in antics and taking away the attention of everyone from the centre point of the scene . . . There seems to be over and over again an absence of discipline and guidance, a want of some kind friend to say when business was excessive and unduly prolonged.'

The pantomime of 1879, *Cinderella*, had to be withdrawn in February as the Vokes family 'struck' when their salaries were not paid. It was when young Harris (he was only twenty-eight) took over that their reign came to an end, although he had to employ them the following Christmas for *Blue Beard*. The new manager was able thereafter to start afresh with his new ideas for pantomime.

AUGUSTUS HARRIS MAKES CHANGES

E. L. Blanchard, while he stayed on at Drury Lane to write the basic pantomime scripts under Harris, was hardly in sympathy with the new trends. As early as 1867 he was complaining they were all 'legs and limelight'.

Harris knew that burlesque, comic opera and, most of all, the music hall were taboo to the sanctimonious middle-class Victorian who more often than not only went to the theatre at Christmas-time to take the children. But, he reasoned, they would come to the Lane and see the artists they would not patronize elsewhere if they were to be seen in pantomime.

His first pantomime without the Vokes family in charge was *Mother Goose and the Enchanted Beauty* in 1880. It opened with a galaxy of young ladies as 'Extraordinary Beings'! Kate Santley, a queen of comic opera from the Alhambra, as Prince Florizel, Arthur Roberts, from the halls, as Dr Syntax teamed with James Fawn and together their topical songs were to become a great success.

The production included two ballets for children, another with the great Emma Palladino as *première danseuse*. Twelve scenes led to the Grand Transformation, 'The Fountain of Love', after which three scenes of Harlequinade culminated in yet another 'Grand Reflected Statue Ballet', again with Palladino.

The following year *Robinson Crusoe*, though as usual credited to Blanchard, was, according to the programme, 'invented, arranged and produced by Augustus Harris'. No wonder poor Blanchard was later to complain bitterly. As Crusoe, Harris cast Fannie Leslie, a famous burlesque artist, Mrs Crusoe was Arthur Roberts, Will Atkins was played by Harry Nicholls, from the Grecian, Charles Lauri was Friday. All the Pirates were female and there were numerous other eye-catching inhabitants of 'The Fairy Glen' and other spectacular scenes, which included two ballets and a Grand Transformation, 'The Fairy Wedding Cake'.

The next year Herbert Campbell, also from the Grecian, joined Harry Nicholls to form a partnership which was to last for some years. Nellie Power was Sindbad and Vesta Tilley, from the halls, was Captain Tra-la-la. The capture of the pantomime citadel by the forces of the halls was complete. The victory was celebrated, as was the success of the British troops in Egypt, with a grand procession of the kings and queens of England from 1066 to date! The two pages inserted in the programme are an instructive and concise history of England, complete with names and dates!

It was an unlucky first night, everything went wrong, but, as usual in true theatrical tradition, all went well in the long run.

Blanchard wrote in his diary:

'To Drury Lane to see *Sindbad* which, though expensively got up, is a very dreary music hall entertainment; and for the misprinting and grossly inter-polated book I am in no way responsible. It was deservedly hissed at various portions—hardly anything done as I intended it, or spoken as I had written: the music hall element is crushing out the rest and the good old fairy-tales never again to be illustrated as they should be.'

Though he still wrote the pantomimes in theory, until 1888, his day was over, as he confided to his diary that Christmas:

'Looking over the ghastly proofs of the Drury Lane annual in which I find my smooth and pointed lines are turned into ragged prose and arrant nonsense, I shall consider the payment due to me an equivalent for the harm done to my literary reputation.'

Blanchard, who died the following year at the age of sixty-eight, was not the only one to complain of the way pantomime had changed. W. Davenport Adams, a critic and theatre historian, wrote in *The Theatre*, February 1882:

'There is, undoubtedly, something to be said in defence of English, or rather British, pantomime, even as it now exists among us. It does one great service to the cause of the dramatic art if it only supplies the monetary surplus which enables a manager to produce the "legitimate" successfully during the remainder of the year. There are many theatrical establishments in this country which are practically kept up by the annual Christmas production and which, but for the money it brings in, would be speedily compelled to close their doors. If there is nothing so expensive, there is certainly nothing—or, at least, "hardly anything"—so lucrative as the yearly pantomime; and, I repeat, if it does nothing more than help to render possible in many localities the maintenance of a "temple of drama," that in itself is something to be grateful for.'

After complaining of the monotony of the subjects chosen, as against the earlier days, he says of those picked:

'They are not only falsified and transmogrified; they are, in too many instances, vulgarised as well.

'Now, to what do we owe this unfortunate, nay painful, feature of pantomime performances? I fear there can be but one answer to the question. We owe it to the music hall element among the performers. I do not mean to say that the ordinary "legitimate" comedian is not very often vulgar; he very often is. I do not say that the fault does not sometimes lie, to a certain extent, with the librettist, who aims too frequently at the gallery. But it is nevertheless to the music hall element that we owe the main portion of that impropriety of word, gesture, and "business" which makes so much of our pantomimes unsuited to the youthful ear and eye—and not only unsuited to the youthful ear and eye, but unpleasant to all people, of whatever age, who possess good taste and feeling. We may say of present day pantomime that the trail of the music hall is over it all. I admit the extreme ability of certain music hall comedians. Nothing could well be cleverer in its way than the singing of Mr. G. H. Macdermott, and the acting of Mr. Herbert Campbell and Mr. Arthur Roberts. I object, however, altogether, to the intrusion of such artists into the domain of pantomime, and I do so because they, and others not so able, bring with them, so to speak, an atmosphere which it is sad to see imported into the theatre. They bring with them not only their songs, which, when offensive in their wording, are sometimes made doubly dangerous by their tunefulness; not only their dances, which are usually vulgar when they are not inane; but their style and manner and "gags." which are generally the most deplorable of all. The objection to music hall artists on the stage is, not only that they help to take the bread out of the mouths of "the profession," which is a minor consideration for the public, but that they have the effect of familiarising general audiences, and children especially, with a style and kind of singing, dancing, and "business" which, however it may be relished by a certain class of the population, ought steadily to be confined to its original habitat. The managers, of course, are very much to blame, for it is by their permission, if not by their desire, that youthful ears are regaled with "W'st, w'st, w'st!" and similar elegant compositions. Such songs as these would not be tolerated by pater familias in his drawing-room, and yet, when he takes his children to the pantomime, they are the most prominent portion of the entertainment. No doubt he and his children can stay way; but in that case it must be openly avowed that pantomime is not *virginibus puerisque*, and if it is not, what, then, is its reason for existing? It will, in that case, have to be confessed that pantomime is dead, and that burlesque of the most deteriorated type has usurped its place.

'There are, indeed, signs that pantomime is being rapidly turned into that species of "burlesque drama" of which Mr. Hollingshead is the chief producer. Mr. Reece's *Aladdin* is virtually a pantomime opening, and the resemblance between the two kinds of entertainment is becoming more striking every day. In both the chief object of the entrepreneur appears to be to put men into women's parts, and women into men's, and, at the same time, to make as great a display as possible of the feminine form. I do not say that this is a creditable object even in one who caters for the public generally; but I am quite sure that it is a vicious object on the part of one who ostensibly provides a holiday entertainment for "the children." A man in woman's clothes cannot but be more or less vulgar, and a woman in male attire, of the burlesque and pantomime description, cannot but appear indelicate to those who have not been hardened to such sights. Any way, it must surely be conceded that the rows of infinitesimally clothed damsels who crowd the pantomime stage are not the sort of spectacle to which it is judicious to introduce the "young idea," especially when it is at that age at which curiosity concerning the forbidden is beginning to display itself. Over and over again must mothers have blushed (if they were able to do so) at the exhibition of female anatomy to which the "highly respectable" pantomime has introduced their children. And so much of this, too, is so utterly and thoroughly gratuitous. There can be charming ballets without reducing the coryphees almost to nudity. I say there can be charming ballets, but how much less is done in this direction than might be done! As a rule how meaningless, how utterly devoid of connection with the story, is this part of a pantomime performance! It is dragged in *vi et armis*, and has rarely even the merit of intrinsic grace. Something might be said, too, as to the monotonous character of the annual transformation scene, which has as little connection with the story as the ballet, and into which scenic artists appear afraid to import the slightest element of originality. When, I wonder, shall we see the last of the unfortunate strapped-up "fairies"? Processions can be so costumed as to be eminently picturesque without impropriety. And, as regards the principals in pantomime, why must the hero always be a woman dressed in tights and tunic? and why must the comic "old woman" always be a man? Have we not plenty of youthful premiers and feminine comedians? Why should professional "old women" and young "walking gentlemen" be banished from pantomime? A genuine "boy prince" would, I think, be an attraction in productions of this sort, and I don't see why the mother of Aladdin should not be enacted by a lady of suitable capacity.'

The intrusion of music hall artists was not the only complaint. Whole acts and specialities were introduced to hold up the action of what story there was left. This, though, was nothing new; the Indian juggler Ramo Samee (who performed before the glass curtain at the Coburg) was introduced into *The Man in The Moon; or, Harlequin Dog-Star* at Drury Lane in 1826. The scene, Vauxhall Gardens 'Birthday Gala and Galaxy of Talent', in itself gave scope for any amount of irrelevant amusement.

Dancing—a *pas de deux* by Harlequin and Columbine, or a *pas seul* by Columbine, had often interrupted the Harlequinade, but the interspersed 'variety' followed the decline of true pantomime after the days of Grimaldi.

Another intrusion was the 'Diorama', a moving panorama of travels at home and abroad, which made its appearance in 1820. These, unfolded yearly, were triumphs of the scene-painter's art. £1,380 was spent on Clarkson Stanfield's 'Moving Diorama', 272 feet long, at Drury Lane in 1823. The painter usually took a 'call' after its display on the opening night and for some years this became part and parcel of pantomime.

As the century grew old the intrusion of 'variety' acts increased. Artists were engaged for their particular speciality, which they introduced with the least provocation or subtlety:

'The Babes asleep; now is the chance
To do my little song and dance.'

Parts were either re-written or completely invented to be in line with the artist's music hall image. Harry Lauder appeared as a Scottish M'Swankey in *Aladdin* at Glasgow in 1905. G. H. Elliot, 'The Chocolate Coloured Coon', was Chocolate in *Mother Hubbard* at Bristol in 1907 and Carlton, 'The Human Hairpin', was Bison Bob, also at Bristol, in 1906.

To this day pantomimes still suffer from this complaint, but in the days of hastily-put-together tours, after the halls were freed in 1911, they became little more than a music hall 'Road Show' with the merest semblance of a pantomime plot. A contrast to the days of carefully rehearsed productions, as shown in two rehearsal scenes at Covent Garden and Drury Lane in 1881 and 1882 (pictures 111 and 112).

Harris's next stroke of luck was to 'discover' Dan Leno, the only other name in pantomime history that has ever been linked with, and become as famous as, that of Grimaldi. Leno, whose real name was Galvin, was born in St Pancras, of poor public-house and minor music hall performers. He was earning money dancing with his uncle, Johnny Danvers, only four weeks his senior, from the age of four! After appearing with his family up and down the country, he won the world championship belt for clog-dancing, in a six-night contest, in 1883. By that time he had also become a comedian and his reputation led George Conquest to engage him as Dame at the Surrey in 1887. His great success there reached the ears of Harris and Conquest released him from his contract for the next year's pantomime to allow him to go to Drury Lane as the Baroness ('The Naughty Aunt') in *Babes in the Wood and Robin Hood and His Merry Men and Harlequin who Killed Cock Robin*. A return to the long Harlequin title; but the Harlequinade was only three short scenes at the tail-end of the evening, though the programme did give the traditional greeting of the Clown (Harry Payne), 'Here we are again'.

This pantomime, the last by Blanchard, with Harris and Nicholls, joined for the first time *The Children in the Wood* plot, founded on the old Norfolk legend, and that of *Robin Hood*, from the old ballad, both of which had been seen separately as pantomimes in the previous decade. It brought together Herbert Campbell and Harry Nicholls as the Babes and Dan Leno as the Dame, with the most statuesque of Principal Boys, Harriet Vernon, as Robin Hood.

Leno and Campbell were to remain the bright particular stars of the Lane until the 1903–04 pantomime, *Humpty Dumpty*, after which, by the next Christmas, they had both died and an era ended. Harris died in 1896 at the early age of forty-four, having gained a knighthood for his civic activities. His work was carried on by Arthur Collins, his stage-manager and successor up to 1920, when the Theatre Royal auditorium was rebuilt. By his day the Harlequinade, or what was left of it, was just an advertisement for 'beverages, boot polish, sausages and crackers'!

Harris remained faithful to his original idea of music hall stars and Vesta Tilley returned as Principal Boy in *Beauty and the Beast* in 1890. Little Tich and Marie Lloyd were in *Humpty Dumpty* in 1891; they were joined by Marie

Loftus for *Little Bo-Peep* the following year. In 1893 Marie Lloyd was Polly Perkins with Little Tich as Man Friday and the Poluski Brothers as Captain and Mate, in *Robinson Crusoe*, with the title rôle played by Ada Blanche, who was Boy at the Lane for six years. The Griffiths Brothers, the Leopolds, Johnny Danvers and Arthur Conquest became regulars at the Lane.

The Australian 'legend', Nellie Stewart, was Ganem in *The Forty Thieves* in 1898, but, though billed, did not appear in *Jack and the Beanstalk* the following year, returning hurriedly home after a backstage *fracas* on Boxing night. Her part was taken at a moment's notice by Mollie Lovell, later replaced by Violet Cameron, another star of burlesque and comic opera.

The writers of the 'nineties include Arthur Sturgess, who collaborated with Collins on several books, and in 1900 J. Hickory Wood came on the scene and remained associated with pantomime at the Lane until 1910. He was also the biographer of Dan Leno, and his scripts did duty up and down the country for many a year.

The most famous of the later Leno–Campbell pantomimes devised by Wood and Collins were *Blue Beard* in 1901, *Mother Goose* in 1902 and *Humpty Dumpty* in 1903.

Of *Blue Beard* the *Playgoer*, a monthly magazine, said:

'As a rule I wouldn't give a fig—to say nothing of a whole boxful—or a brass button, or two pins, to witness a pantomime. I say *to witness a pantomime*. But there is one Xmas annual, to see which for twelve consecutive years I have cheerfully paid for two stalls, and that is the imposing spectacle, and more or less funny pantomime at Old Drury. Rather would I miss the sixteen-hour-boiled pudding, which always follows the turkey, or some other wretched bird —I say *some other wretched bird*—on December 25th, than not go to Drury Lane. But to the point, which, in this instance, is the pantomime.

'On a Monday afternoon, just fourteen days ago (there is a familiarity about the sound of "fourteen days" I do not like, but—no matter!) I made the wife of my bosom happy (I believe "my bosom" is correct, although she is, of course, equally the wife of the rest of her husband—I say *the rest of her husband*) by conveying her, with reasonable speed, to the freshly painted, and newly up-holstered National Theatre, in grimy, gloomy Drury Lane. Strange contrast! I say *strange contrast*.

'How we chuckled as we gazed at the human stream, which resembled the good old sea serpent, as it filtered its way into the big building.

' "Lucky you booked our seats four weeks ago, Jack!"

' "Yes, dear! I'm told the receipts are nearly, and sometimes quite, a thousand pounds a day; and some are anxiously enquiring for seats for the Easter holidays. I say *for the Easter holidays*."

'Mingling with the mass, and after refusing to purchase "Ho-fisshul pro-grammes" from half a dozen local inhabitants who might have done better if they had taken a bath—I say *if they had taken a bath*—before commencing their sale, we finally flopped into our seats, to drink in, as it were, the lively music emanating from Jimmy Glover's glorious band.

'The pantomime, I find, is this year divided into three sections, with two intervals for Irish or Scotch. I say *for Irish or Scotch*.

'The curtain rose on the meeting of the Four Winds, a windy spot, with a wind mill, and amid much shrieking and whistling (I quite expected to see the man with the big drum, and all the wind instruments, blown from their places in the orchestra) the usual plot was concocted, including the making of a magic fan which was to fan the beautiful Fatima's curiosity. And then the show started. I say *then the show started*.

'In the "Slave Market" we met Blue Beard the millionaire (but in reality, that artful music hall favourite, Herbert Campbell); Blue Beard's six plain wives—he loved them once but couldn't love them twice; Shacabac, [Fred Zola] a short servant, paid to see Blue Beard's jokes, but, being short-sighted, laughed at them in the wrong place; Hassarac, [Laurence Caird] a long servant, paid to give away Blue Beard's money, but, being deaf, never heard anyone ask for it; and Mustapha, [Fred Emney] who diddled Blue Beard into buying six girl slaves—all domesticated, and excellent ping-pong performers—I say *excellent ping-pong performers*—for a lot of shekels and a glass of sherbet.

'Now No. 6 of Mustapha's little lot was none other than his *eldest* daughter Anne, *alias* Dan—the King's jester—whose surname is Leno; and then the fun began.

'Says Blue Beard: "There's some mistake, I never ordered a *remnant*."

' "But," says Anne, "tut, tut! I'm the very wife for *you*—a millionaire—who don't know what to do with your money, and I'll do it, see?"

'Before the bargain was concluded, Mustapha's youngest, the fascinating Fatima, [Julia Franks] was thrown in for more shekels, as a sort of makeweight, and followed by Selim, [Elaine Ravensberg] her sorrowing sweetheart, the whole crowd were next found on Blue Beard's vessel.

'Now Selim attempted to save Fatima from his rival, but failing, jumped overboard alone, to be cast up, anon, on the lovely island of ferns, where the aforesaid magic fan is manufactured. Here real water was falling, and flying fairies, and every variety and shade of green bird and beetle combined to make, well—one of those scenes for which Arthur Collins is famous (I say *for which Arthur Collins is famous*), and which is always followed by a thunderclap of applause.

'In Part II., Blue Beard had conducted the unwilling Fatima to his castle, where he left her with his keys, and the well known precaution regarding the mysterious chamber. Then came the fanning of Fatima's curiosity, and, with the assistance of Dan Leno—I mean Anne—she used the forbidden key, which not only turned the lock, but turned *blue*—and then—

'A shriek for help from Fatima brought Selim, who had traced her to the castle, to her side, and Anne was left with the heads of Blue Beard's six ugly wives, which were hanging on hooks after the manner of the "Aunt Sallies" we used to knock down for cokernuts. These heads, mark you, had no bodies (although they had been "somebodies"), but they still had their tongues, and could still talk. They were female heads. I say *they were female heads*. A monster seventh head, [Arthur Conquest] which would have brought business to a standstill if it had strolled down the Strand, waddled round, and, with Anne, had a little argument on its own account.

'The triumph of the Magic Fan was then celebrated, the vast stage being filled with fans of every conceivable pattern, size, and colour. They were carried by Chinese mandarins, gorgeously dressed Indians, dainty Dresden shepherdesses, funny little Japs, sunny Spanish dancers, and more flying fairies.

'This was a second scene that elicited a mighty thunderclap of approval.

'When, in Part III., Blue Whiskers had returned from his travels, Selim and Sister Leno got up a little *Hamlet* scene to prick his conscience, to "wring his withers and make the galled jade wince." This put Mr. B. into a dangerous mood, and caused him to want everybody's head, but the good fairy bobbed up again, and Blue Beard, convinced that he hadn't a leg to stand on, with his rival in the field, just "climbed down."

'The final scene, the magic (spiral) staircase, surrounded by a mighty, marching, singing, trumpet blowing, and magnificently costumed army—a mass of dazzling splendour—brought applause which might have been heard in Fleet Street. I say *might have been heard in Fleet Street*.

'Once again Arthur Collins, who manages everything, and J. Hickory Wood, who, with Arthur, supplied the book, and J. M. Glover, who arranged the music, and Bruce Smith, Caney, Emden, and others who painted the scenery; and Comelli, who designed the costumes, and Carlo Coppi and John D'Auban, who arranged the ballets, are triumphant.

'Once again Old Drury has played the ace of trumps, and with the production of *Blue Beard* reigns supreme in the kingdom of pantomime. To those who have not been, I say "Go!" Until then don't believe me. I say *don't believe me*.'

The Harlequinade had Whimsical Walker for Clown but was further reduced to two scenes.

The only challenge to the Lane in the West End of London was Oscar Barrett at the Lyceum, while Irving was away from his theatre. His *Cinderella* with Ellaline Terriss, in 1893, became such a success that it crossed the Atlantic after the London run but, once again, did not establish pantomime on Broadway, even in its new form.

Barrett followed this with *Santa Claus* in 1894 and *Robinson Crusoe* in 1895. He was called in at the Lane after Harris's death in 1896 to produce *Aladdin* before Collins took control.

Gerald Forsyth, a devotee of pantomime, held Barrett in high esteem:

'He paid much attention to the musical side of his productions, being a trained musician. The son of a musician, he began his career, when quite a boy, as a violinist in the orchestra at the Grecian Theatre under Conquest. Here he gained much knowledge in the art of Pantomime production. He later became musical director at the Grecian, composing much of the music. Thence to the Crystal Palace, where he produced over twenty Pantomimes, on to Manchester, and in 1892 he began his West End career at the Olympic, also producing Pantomimes in the provinces. He eventually retired to his home at St. Margaret's Bay, where he died in 1941, at the great age of ninety-five. He always made a feature of the Harlequinade and, in Charles Lauri, also an expert animal impersonator, he had a first rate clown.'

While the suburban theatres were busy, each with its own individual production, so were the provincial centres, often three or more pantomimes being produced in the larger towns.

At Christmas 1900/01 *The Stage* lists two West End pantomimes, at Drury Lane and at the London Hippodrome, (which had opened that year with a mixture of circus, variety and spectacular water shows). Around London there were twenty-four resident productions and thirty-eight in the provinces. The interchange of books, scenery and casts around the country year by year constituted a formidable 'industry'. From the earlier days 'books' of pantomimes were published for sale, or given as souvenirs, in the theatre, in much the same way as libretti in the opera houses. These books, often well illustrated, provide a guide to the tastes and quality of the authorship of the day. As late as Christmas 1938/9, at the Lyceum, the last stronghold in London of 'traditional' pantomime, the programme was still accompanied by a 'book of words'.

The provinces became famous for their Principal Boys, drawn mostly from the music halls or musical comedy and light opera. These included stars like Ada Reeve, who had first appeared in pantomime before the age of five in 1878 at the Pavilion, Whitechapel, famous for its pantomimes. She played her first Boy in 1892 and, after her music hall beginnings, went into musical comedy under George Edwardes at the Gaiety in *The Shop Girl* in 1894. From then on her contracts usually allowed her to play an annual pantomime engagement. She was last seen in pantomime as Aladdin, in Australia, in 1924.

Others, like Zena and Phyllis Dare, Dorothy Ward and Maidie Andrews, are alive and remembered today with affection by an older generation, who collected dozens of their Picture Post Cards. Provincial centres like Liverpool, Manchester, Birmingham and Bristol vied with each other and have handed down the results of their efforts on Picture Post Cards. The series of the *Cinderella* at the Shakespeare Theatre, Liverpool, in 1907, give a good idea of what provincial productions were like (pictures 157, 158, 159, 160).

Of this pantomime *The Stage* reported:

'Fraser Street is shaking with laughter. Unembarrassed by gorgeous scenery, opulence of costuming, richness of staging, or splendours of ballet, the company go on their merry way with free hands and ceaseless, untiring humour. The pantomime of *Cinderella* is just sufficiently well mounted to please the general taste. Its most ardent admirer will not claim for it any embarrassment of riches in this direction, but what there is makes a sufficiently picturesque background for the comedians to disport themselves in front of, and they certainly do this royally. There has been a gathering of scenery from all quarters, for there are examples by Thos. Holmes, Stafford Hall, E. Gremani, A. Terrance, R. C. Oldham, and D. G. Hall; and, as variety is charming, in the present housing of *Cinderella* there should be nothing to complain of. The main feature of this present story is that dealing with Baron de Debtington and his portly four-fifths of a wife. Comical contrasts in stature have served in stage pieces for many years, so that, although not a novelty, the diminutive husband, with the satirical name of Hercules, and the massive wife, christened Tiny, obviously serve for great fun. In these two parts we have Mr. George French and Mr. Tom Conway respectively. A better choice could scarcely have been made. Mr. Conway is noted for a broad, rich style of humour, almost plethoric with comicality. Active or passive in his work, the results are the same—laughter, free, full, and spontaneous. The current of his contagious merriment is never cut off while he is on the stage, and Conway and convulsive mirth are likely to become synonymous in Liverpool. In the wretched, woe-begone figure and suffering countenance of the shrunken Hercules Mr. French stands a monument —diminutive only in figure—of fun. He presents this haggard creature with genuine comedy, plays him with real touches of art, and there is nothing in the interpretation suggestive of the superficial extravagances of mere pantomime. Another happy hit is the Dandini of Mr. George Lashwood. We are all familiar with the debonaire style of this well-known comedian, and it is delightful to find here that he has easily adapted himself to the necessities of the part, and is quite an integral figure of the picture. He sings his songs with that flowing grace and smoothness which is characteristic of him, and he sends them swinging to the audience with irresistible attraction. His first song is "The Twi-twilight," sung with a setting of lovers in that romantic part of the evening; "Put me among the girls"; and "The best girl," this last "worked" with a charming little creature, who helps the comedian with a zest and spirit which rouse the audience to great enthusiasm. A very enjoyable Cinderella is seen in Miss Alice Russon, who has a delightfully *naïve* manner and is refreshingly sweet; a pretty singer and a pleasant little comedienne. Miss Madoline Rees plays the Prince with quite a stately grace, and proves an adept in the art of suggesting the romantic male. A cordial welcome is given to Miss Nellie Christie, whose former triumph in Prince of Wales's pantomime here is not forgotten. She infuses a good deal of humour into her part of Araminta, as does clever Miss Murcelle Langley with the other sister, Elvira. Miss Ellaline Thorne shines brightly as the Duke of Whistbridge. One of the smartest appearances and work is that of the Capers of Mr. Barry Lupino. His comicalities are both acrobatic and histrionic, and he is equally clever in both. Miss Marie West is a delightful Fairy Godmother, and quite a charm of the pantomime. The Doreen Girls supply some graceful and expert dancing. The processions and ballets have been arranged by Bertha Valentine. The whole production owes much to Stanley Rogers, author and producer. His book is clearly and crisply written, and is fully deserving the close attention the company give it. The musical values of the pantomime have been provided by Harry Richardson and George M. Saker. This is the fourth year of service which the latter clever composer and director has given to Shakespeare pantomime. The melodies are rich, and the variety of the music is in the best possible taste, whilst the chorus and processional writing is full of attractive and inspiriting quality.'

With the tragic deaths of both Herbert Campbell and Dan Leno in 1904, the Lane was forced to look for new stars. Harry Randall, from the halls, took over as Dame in *The White Cat* in 1904. Walter Passmore, from the D'Oyly Carte Company at the Savoy, was the Baroness in *Cinderella* in 1905, with an Anglo-French comedian, Harry Fragson, as 'Dandigny'. The Ugly Sisters were female. It had become 'traditional' that, if there was a 'Baroness' (Dame), the 'Sisters' would be 'girls', but if the Baron was a widower, then he had 'male' daughters. The Principal Boy of the period was Queenie Leighton. In 1910 George Graves became Dame and remained at the Lane for five seasons. The influence of musical comedy was becoming felt as much as that of the halls. Agnes Fraser was Robin Hood in 1907, Violet Loraine Hilarion (in *Hop o' my Thumb*) in 1911, Florence Smithson the Princess, in *The Sleeping Beauty*, in 1912 and 1913. Old pantomime names were still to be found, a new generation of Lupinos, Barry and Stanley, joined their father, George, who was Clown in 1912. The name Vokes still crops up, and Arthur Conquest was there almost continuously from 1901 to 1920.

The biggest innovation came in 1912, and it turned out to be twofold. Firstly a completely new version of *The Sleeping Beauty* was written by George R. Sims, C. H. Bovill and Arthur Collins. It included several unfamiliar characters including Puck (Renée Mayer), to say nothing of two detectives, Blake and Holmes, but the Prince, Auriol, was played by a man, Wilfrid Douthitt, a well-known concert singer, which caused traditionalists to rise in their wrath! The following year came the second innovation, the pantomime had a sequel, *The Sleeping Beauty Re-Awakened* with the same principals, to be followed the next Christmas, after war had broken out in 1914, with yet another *The Sleeping Beauty*, this time *Beautified*. Now, though, the Principal Boy was Bertram Wallis, the famous *jeune premier* from Daly's.

There was to be another war and a gap of forty-three years, until 1957, before London again saw a boy 'Boy'!

A NEW 'TRADITION'

As the war progressed pantomime still bore out the slogan 'Keep on carrying on', at the Lane. *Puss in Boots*, 1915, *Puss in New Boots*, 1916, *Aladdin*, 1917, *Babes in the Wood*, 1918, and a peace-time *Cinderella* in 1919. The successful run of a dramatized version of Robert Hitchens' *The Garden of Allah* was not interrupted in 1920, and the previous year's *Cinderella* was put on at Covent Garden, where pantomime had not been staged for thirty-two years. It ran for only sixty-five performances. The following Christmas Drury Lane was being re-constructed; then, with the success of the great American musicals of the 'twenties, no pantomime was seen there again until a *Sleeping Beauty* in 1929. It was Julian Wylie who was responsible for its return. A great pantomime producer, he was credited up to that time with sixty-five productions. He came back to the Lane for the *Cinderella* of 1935 and *Jack and the Beanstalk* in 1936.

After that, but for a hastily conceived *Babes in the Wood* in 1938, 'King Panto' has not again reigned at the Lane. Stars from all spheres of the theatre graced these years; Lilian Davies, Phyllis Neilson-Terry, Fay Compton and Binnie Hale among them.

At the Garden, opera and ballet were not displaced except for *Red Riding Hood* in 1938, with Patricia Burke as Boy and Nelson Keys as Dame, under the direction of another famous pantomime producer, Francis Laidler. In the scene 'Meadowsweet Lane' he introduced 'The Lambeth Walk', by special permission of Lupino Lane, from the current success *Me and My Girl* at the Victoria Palace.

Less spectacular, but more traditional pantomime, that was less reliant on the music halls, was maintained under the Melville brothers at the Lyceum. The old theatre, the home of Irving, which had stood since 1834, had been pulled down except for the outer walls in 1903 and replaced with a red plush and gilt music hall. The new hall failed dismally, and after several tenants was taken by the Melvilles as a home for domestic and historical Melo-Drama (in the real sense of the word), with annual pantomimes from 1910 until the theatre was closed shortly after the *Queen of Hearts* of 1938/9. A long record of popular pantomime, with its own particular stars and flavour; to the end a mockery of a Harlequinade was given, but it was played to an audience leaving the theatre to catch the last bus or train, while a pathetic Clown and his followers threw Tom Smith's crackers at a departing public. A sad end to what had once been the mainstay of pantomime.

Ironically a Harlequinade turned up as a prologue, of all things, at the Palladium before *Cinderella* in 1953, its last gasp, though its obituary had been written by no less a person than George Bernard Shaw, who, in *The Era*, 30 December 1937, under the heading 'Grimaldi is dead, why not bury him?' said:

'The Christmas Pantomime, being our most fantastic and fairylandish form of theatrical art, should never be allowed to get into a groove; yet there is no sort of public entertainment that has been more hopelessly stuck in a groove for a century past.

'It is just a hundred years since the death of the great Joey Grimaldi, who created a sort of clown peculiar to himself, as Dundreary was peculiar to Sothern, Robert Macaire to Frédèric Lemaitre, or as the screen tramp is to Charlie Chaplin.

'Now nothing in the theatre is more tiresome and futile than attempts by later actors to reproduce these idiosyncratic masterpieces. Sham Chaplins are not in the least funny, no matter how industriously they work the bowler hat, the little cane, and the shuffling gait. Sham Dundrearys are only silly; and sham Grimaldis are the worst of all stage impostures because they have spoiled so many pantomimes.

'I have seen dozens of them; and not one has amused me since I was a very small child and thought it all real.

'Once I saw a good pantaloon—one of the Hulines—but he discarded tradition and played gravely as an old marquis in a court dress of extreme elegance.

'I recall one brilliant harlequin, Teddy Royce, a first-rate burlesque actor and dancer. And I admit that a pantomime once kept me shrieking with laughter for half an hour and in thorough good humour for the rest of the evening. Its subject was *Sinbad the Sailor* and what made me laugh so shamelessly was an outrageously vulgar exploitation of the humours of sea-sickness. The theatre was the Britannia in Hoxton; and the audience consisted mostly of 4,000 factory girls who threw boxes of sweets to their favourite performers and screamed frantically if they were picked up by the wrong person.

'All the politer pantomimes have bored and disgusted me.

'Sham Grimaldi was dying an intolerably slow death all the time.

'*Peter Pan* was an attempt to get Christmas pieces out of their groove. *Androcles and the Lion* was another.

'I have sometimes trifled with the notion that if only Grimaldi and Dan Leno and Herbert Campbell had never been born, we might be able to get back to the elegant fairy tales of the eighteenth century extravaganzas, with or without their transformation of the principals into a really dainty quartet of harlequin and columbine, rascally acrobat comedian and *père noble*. But we need to go forward, not backward.

'As to the notion that the theatre has lost touch with the lives and problems of the man in the street, people would not write such nonsense if they could remember the theatre as it was when I was a beginner.

'Do they really think that the plays of Mr. St John Ervine, Mr. Priestley and Mr. Bridie are further from the lives and problems of our playgoers than the plays of Tom Taylor and the endless adaptations from the French which were the West End stock-in-trade fifty years ago? If so, they should have their pens taken away from them. Historical criticism is not their job.'

It was not for nothing that Mrs Patrick Campbell affectionately called Shaw 'Joey' after Grimaldi.

During the years a new 'repertory-theatre' pantomime came into being. Simply-written stories for actors, with songs they could sing, aimed at the local children and exploiting the 'traditional' pantomime scenes, 'the Schoolroom', 'the Kitchen', 'the Nursery' or 'Dressing for the Ball'. With the decline of the music hall stars and their 'personal' songs, 'free' songs were sung and plugged in every conceivable situation. Music publishers fought to get their latest ballads and comedy songs into productions up and down the country.

Topical crazes were still featured. In 1920, Will Evans as Dame in *Cinderella* at the Lane sang 'All the girls are busy knitting jumpers', joined by the Chorus, both male and female, doing likewise! The same year Phyllis Dare, in *Aladdin* at the Hippodrome, sang 'I'm forever blowing bubbles' while both Chorus and audience experimented with Bibby's Bouncing Bubble Powder! Bonzo, Felix, Teddy Tail, Pip, Squeak and Wilfred, all found a place in a topical Pantomime Zoo, and the Dame still satirized the latest fads of female fashion. London was able to maintain at least two pantomimes each year in the centre of town between the wars. The London Palladium, relying heavily on music hall artists in the 'twenties, under Charles Gulliver, filled the theatre twice daily. The London Hippodrome staged Julian Wylie productions with famous pantomime names, like Phyllis Dare, Nellie Wallace, Shaun Glenville, Lupino Lane, Wee Georgie Wood, George Robey, and many others, but it was in the provinces that the Salbergs, the Littlers, Laidler and Tom Arnold were keeping the traditions alive.

When the next war loomed on the horizon pantomime did not go underground and, though the suburban theatres had dwindled, the variety halls still had touring pantomimes playing four or five dates around the circuits, and resident productions at Wimbledon, Hammersmith, Streatham Hill and Golders Green were still to be seen. When later some of these theatres ceased activity pantomime, not to be denied, went to the local town hall or cinema. Gradually, though, as tastes changed and television gained its stranglehold on live entertainment, so pantomimes dwindled around the outskirts.

In the West End Emile Littler kept the flag flying at the Coliseum and the London Casino, both during and after the war, and Bertram Montague followed old traditions at the Princes Theatre with Hy Hazel as a perfect Principal Boy in the old style. Pantomime returned to the London Palladium under Val Parnell and this became the only stronghold left in the West End maintaining the variety tradition from 1948 to 1960, but during this time the first big innovation for years was to be seen. Norman Wisdom, a variety comedian, played Aladdin in 1957, and Boys became boys once again.

The next change in the pantomime scene came the following year at the Coliseum, when Harold Fielding put on Rogers and Hammerstein's *Cinderella*. This had been written for television in America as a fairy-story musical to star Julie Andrews in 1957. For London it was turned into a pantomime, complete with all the traditional trappings added by Ronnie Wolfe.

The greatest innovation was a complete score and lyrics as in a musical, and a completely designed production by Loudon Sainthill. It was directed by Freddie Carpenter, who since 1951 had been directing pantomimes in the provinces, often four at a time at the same Christmas! The cast included Tommy Steele as Buttons, Yana as Cinderella and Jimmy Edwards as the King, with Kenneth Williams and Ted Durante as the Ugly Sisters. It was revived in 1960 at the Adelphi Theatre.

At Christmas 1959, at the Coliseum, *Aladdin*, a similar production with music and lyrics by Cole Porter, was produced, with Bob Monkhouse as Aladdin. A new 'tradition' had been founded.

The Palladium followed the trend with integrated productions within the older trappings, drawing on the variety and pop world for its artists. From 1961 to 1970 Leslie Macdonald and Bernard Delfont, with Robert Nesbitt directing, were responsible for the Christmas productions.

After Norman Wisdom in 1957, the male Principal Boy became established, with Edmund Hockridge (1958), Frankie Vaughan (1962), Cliff Richard (1964), Frank Ifield (1965), Peter Gilmore (1966), Englebert Humperdinck (1967), Jimmy Tarbuck (1968), Tommy Steele (1969) and Edward Woodward (1972) among their ranks, drawn from all walks of the theatre.

The ageless Dorothy Ward, Prince of Principal Boys, capitulated and played her last Dick Whittington at Liverpool in 1957, bringing to an end the long partnership with her husband Shaun Glenville.

For one disastrous year the West End was without a pantomime, when it was decided to put on a 'Space-Age Musical' with Charlie Drake, called *The Man in the Moon*, in 1963, but pantomime survived and returned in triumph the following year to the Palladium, where Louis Benjamin has been in charge since 1971.

The provinces remained more or less faithful to the older style of pantomime and a 'female' Principal Boy is still to be found up and down the country, sharing the limelight with the pop 'Boy' Principal.

For some years Danny La Rue had been making his name in pantomime away from London, and drew West End audiences to Golders Green before he burst upon the metropolis in *Queen Passionella and the Sleeping Beauty* at the Saville Theatre in 1968. It was a 'new' pantomime, devised by Bryan Blackburn and Freddie Carpenter, who also directed, and contained all the best of 'traditional' pantomime with a 'new look'. *Queen of Hearts* at Manchester, a pantomime by the same team, was produced in 1972. No doubt London will see this anon.

However much one applauds the new trend to a fully designed and integrated production, the old fashioned pantomime, with dresses 'improvised' by the Dame and the introduced popular song, will be missed by an older generation.

If the undergraduates look younger when one returns to one's *alma mater*, if one notices how young the police seem to look, or if pantomime is not so good as it was, this is a sure sign of age!

We can only add, in the closing words of *Dick Whittington* at the Lyceum Theatre, 1925:

> 'In your hands our fate now lies
> To all our faults please close your eyes.'

Acknowledgements

Pantomime has been the subject of annual magazine articles from the earliest days of popular journalism, but far fewer books have been written on this exclusively British subject than would be imagined.

Charles Dickens ('Boz') edited *Memoirs of Grimaldi* (1838) and there were the reminiscences of pantomime writers like Dibdin, Planché, Blanchard, etc., which cover the whole spectrum of the theatre of their times, not exclusively early pantomime. John Weaver surprisingly wrote a *History of Mimes and Pantomimes* in 1728. Andrew Halliday wrote about Clowns in *Comical Fellows* (1893), and to an 'All About Series' in 1891 Leopold Wagner contributed *The Pantomimes and All About Them*, but the first full history did not appear until R. J. Broadbent wrote *A History of Pantomime* in 1901. The classic work of M. Wilson Disher, *Clowns and Pantomimes* (1925), ranges far and wide over the whole subject of *Commedia dell'Arte* and pantomime.

The three books on pantomime by A. E. Wilson, *Christmas Pantomime* (1934), *Pantomime Pageant* (1946) and *The Story of Pantomime* (1949), though chatty journalistic reading, are full of misleading 'facts', the fruits of a loving journalist's enthusiasm without due basic research. Thelma Niklaus explored the character of Harlequin with great skill in *Harlequin Phoenix* in 1956, but, after Richard Findlater had written *Grimaldi, King of Clowns*, a new biography, in 1955 and re-edited the *Memoirs* in 1968, it was left to an American professor, David Mayer III, to make a full exploration of English Regency Pantomime from 1806–36, in *Harlequin in His Element*, published by Harvard and Oxford Universities. The first full dress nod in this direction by the academic world, though numerous Dissertations and Papers have appeared in learned journals, notably 'The Infancy of English Pantomime 1716–1723' by Virginia P. Scott (*Educational Theatre Journal* 1972).

We have tried to tell the story of pantomime and make its composition clear by pictorial means. We have had to dig deep into the grass roots of its history and, in doing so, have found many a slip in the work of our predecessors (which we have now, we hope, cleared up), to say nothing of the confused thinking of our juniors in mixing burlesque and extravaganza with panto-mime! One is bedevilled at every turn by the label 'tradition', which has grown out of 'custom' and lost its original meaning on the way.

In our search for the truth we have been helped, as always, by the staff of the Enthoven Collection at the Victoria and Albert Museum, led by George Nash. We must extend to Tony Latham, as usual, our devoted thanks for his help at all times, far beyond the call of duty. We have also drawn on the Harry Beard Collection, now under the wing of the Enthoven Collection at the V. and A. Owners of original pictures, the Garrick Club, the British Museum and T. Osborne Robinson, have been generous in allowing us to reproduce their treasures. We also thank Waldo Lanchester, who brought his 'Pantorama' to our notice and allowed us to include it; William Bell and Alfred Todd, the princes of Picture Post Card collectors, who both gave us of their time and resources from opposite ends of the British Isles.

We also thank the unknown admirer of Dorothy Ward who sent her the verses 'Principal Boy', and Dorothy herself, for letting us use them and for accepting our dedication.

We have also to thank the Press Office of London Transport, Douglas Byng, Harold Fielding, Jack Hanson, Robert Palmer and Mike Regan for their patience and kindness in so many ways.

The Society of Authors has allowed us to use the Bernard Shaw article, now appearing in a book for the first time, and we thank Dan Laurence for bringing it to our notice.

The work of the following photographers is represented by kind permission of the Harold Fielding office and the press office of the London Palladium: Dezo Hoffman, Nos. 239, 242, 243, 247, 248; Matthews, Nos. 234, 238; Barnet Saidman, F.I.B.P., Nos. 236, 237; Kevin Scott, No. 246.

David Mayer and Paul Sawyer (who is writing a life of Rich), have both allowed us to draw upon their work.

On the purely physical side of the manuscript, as usual Vera Seaton-Reid provided material assistance, but all credit must go to Mary Quinnell, who not only coped with us and our notes, but this time the index also, a truly monu-mental task! The alert eyes of Derek Priestley and Joan Waldegrave at our Publishers must be acknowledged with appreciation as must the patience of Peter Ireland with the complicated artwork.

Lastly, and most especially, our sincere thanks to Danny La Rue for his foreword.

RAYMOND MANDER
JOE MITCHENSON

The Drury Lane posters reproduced on the end-papers are:

Cinderella	by The Beggarstaff Brothers	1895
Aladdin	” Dudley Hardy	1896
Blue Beard	” Colliford	1901
The White Cat	” John Hassell	1904
Puss in New Boots	” Louis Wain	1916
The Babes in the Wood	” G. L. Stampa	1918

[48]

Indexes

PANTOMIMES ILLUSTRATED
(with theatre and date: London, unless otherwise stated)

[51]

TOWNS AND THEATRES REPRESENTED

ACTORS APPEARING IN PANTOMIME

PRINTS AND DRAWINGS, ETC.

ARTISTS AND DESIGNERS

MISCELLANEOUS

'We've brought our story to an end,
For our success, we must on you depend.
May we dear friends, you kind applause exhort,
To send our vessel safely into port.'

Robinson Crusoe,
Prince of Wales Theatre, Liverpool 1882.

1. John Rich as Harlequin in a scene from *The Necromancer; or, Harlequin Dr Faustus*. Lincoln's Inn Fields Theatre, December 1723. A contemporary watercolour by an unknown artist in the British Museum. One of the earliest known scenes from a pantomime, and one of Rich's first successes of which the *Daily Journal*, 9 January 1724, said:

> 'The Concourse of People to see it was so exceeding great, that many hundreds were obliged to go back again, as not being able to gain Admittance; the Entertainment was wonderful satisfactory to the Audience, as exceeding all the Legerdemain that has hitherto been performed on the Stage.'

A similar pantomime by John Thurmond (who had been with Rich) was staged at Drury Lane Theatre a month earlier; another version of the Faust legend was seen at the Little Theatre in the Haymarket.

The popularity of conjuring and trickery brought to London by Signor Faux and the development of stage transformation scenery combined to find in the Faust story an ideal subject which at Lincoln's Inn 'induced the vulgar to believe Mr Rich was a real sorcerer.'

Harlequin Dr Fauſtus in the Necromancer.

RICH, THE HARLEQUIN.

Thank you Genteels. Theſe ſtunning Claps declare,
How Wit corporeal is y.^e darling Care.
See what it is the crouding Audience draws
While Wilks no more but Fauſtus gains Applauſe.

3. A satirical engraving published in 1724, by William Hogarth, titled 'Masquerades and Operas; Burlington Gate.' It shows the popularity of pantomime, conjuring, masquerades and the newly introduced Italian opera driving the legitimate drama from the theatre.

In *The Works of William Hogarth* by John Nichols, 1837, the print is described:

'On a board is a display of the words "Long Room. Faux's dexterity of hand." On the opposite corner is the figure of Harlequin, pointing to a label, on which is written, "Dr Faustus is here". This was a pantomime performed to crowded houses throughout two seasons.

'In this Print all the figures have a strong resemblance to those of Callot; and the follies of the town are very severely satirized, by the representation of multitudes, properly habited, crowding to the Masquerade, Opera, and Pantomime; whilst the works of our greatest Dramatic Writers are trundled through the streets in a wheel-barrow, and cried as waste paper for shops; among these may be distinguished Shakespeare, Ben Johnson, Dryden, Congreve, Otway, Farquhar, and Addison. In the first copy of this Print, instead of Ben Jonson's name on a label, we have "Pasquin, No. XI". This was a periodical paper, published in 1722–5; and the number specified is particularly severe on Operas, &c.

'Some verses (not always the same) are found under the first impressions of the Print. Under the earliest impressions of 1724 these verses appear:

> Could now dumb Faustus, to reform the age,
> Conjure up Shakespeare's or Ben Johnson's Ghost,
> They'd blush for shame, to see the *English* Stage
> Debauch'd by Fool'ries, at so great a cost.
>
> What would their manes say, should they behold
> Monsters and masquerades, where useful plays
> Adorn'd the fruitful theatre of old.
> And rival wits contended for the bays?'

4. 'A just view of the British Stage, or three heads are better than one. Scene Newgate.' 1724. Another of Hogarth's satires on the popularity of pantomime.

Horace Walpole in his Catalogue, thus describes this plate: 'Booth, Wilkes, and Cibber, contriving a Pantomime; a Satire on Farces.

'This Print represents the Rehearsing a new Farce that will include ye two famous Entertainments *Dr Faustus* & *Harlequin Sheppard*, to which will be added Scaramouch Jack Hall the Chimney Sweeper's Escape from Newgate through ye Privy, with ye comical Humours of Ben Jonson's Ghost. Concluding with the Hay-Dance perform'd in ye Air by ye Figures A.B.C. assisted by Ropes from ye Muses. Note, there are no Conjurors concern'd in it as ye ignorant imagine. The Bricks, Rubbish &c. will be real, but the Excrements upon Jack Hall will be made of Chew'd Ginger-bread to prevent offence. *Vivat Rex.* It may be added, that Mr Devoto was Scene-painter either to Drury Lane or Lincoln's Inn Fields, and also to Goodman's Fields Theatre; that the ropes mentioned in the inscription are nothing other than halters, suspended over the heads of the three Managers; and that the labels issuing from their respective mouths convey the following characteristic words. The airy Wilkes, who dangles the effigy of Punch, exclaims, 'Poor R--ch! faith, I *pitty* him.' The Laureate Cibber, who is amusing himself with playing with Harlequin, invokes the Muse painted on the ceiling, 'Assist, ye sacred Nine!' And the solemn Booth, letting down the figure of Jack Hall into the *forica*, is most tragically exclaiming, with an oath, 'Ha! this will do.' At the same instant Ben Jonson's ghost is rising through the stage, and insulting a pantomime statue fallen from its base. Over the figure of Hall is suspended a parcel of waste paper, consisting of leaves from 'The Way of the World'. A pamphlet on the table exhibits a Print of Jack Sheppard in confinement. A dragon is also preparing to fly; a dog thrusts his head out of the kennel; a flask acquires motion by machinery, &c. The countenances of Tragedy and Comedy on each side of the stage, are concealed by the bills for 'Harlequin Dr Faustus', 'Harlequin Sheppard', &c.

5. 'Rich's Triumphal Entry.' Hogarth's satire 1732. The new theatre in Covent Garden, built out of the profits of panto-mime, is ready.

'This Plate represents the removal of Rich, and his Scenery, Authors, Actors, &c., from Lincoln's Inn Fields, to the new House. The scene is the Area of Covent Garden, across which, leading toward the door of the Theatre, is a long procession, consisting of a cart loaded with thunder and lightning, Performers, &c.; and at the head of them Mr Rich (invested with the skin of the famous Dog in *Perseus and Andromeda*) riding with his Mistress in a chariot driven by Harlequin, and drawn by Satyrs.'

6. John Rich (1692–1761) as Harlequin. An engraving from a watercolour by an unknown artist, 1753. The watercolour shows Rich in the year of his last appear-ance with a full mask which is not in the engraving, but on comparison it appears that the engraver has turned the mask into Rich's face showing Harlequin maskless!

7. Rich as 'Don Jumpedo in the character of Harlequin jumping down his own throat', a scene from *The Royal Chase; or, Harlequin Skeleton.* Covent Garden Theatre, 1749.

London was hoaxed by the Duke of Montague, who wanted to test the credulity of the public. It was advertised that a person, among other feats of conjuring, would get into a quart bottle on the stage of the Little Theatre in the Haymarket. When he did not turn up to a full house the audience grew restive and a riot ensued. This event was satirized by Rich in a pantomime shortly after. He advertised:

'Lately arrived from Italy, Sig. *Capitello Jumpedo*, a surprizing dwarf, no taller than a common tavern tobacco pipe; who can perform many wonderful equilibres, on the slack or tight rope: Likewise he'll transform his body in above ten thousand different shapes and postures; and after he has diverted the spectators two hours and a half, he will open his mouth wide, and jump down his own throat.'

8. Rich as Don Jumpedo, another version of the same scene:

'Howe'er impossible the Feat may seem,
Which first gave Rise to the delusive Scheme;
What *foreign* Apes in frolic, frantic Wit
Wou'd pass upon the *Boxes* and the *Pit*;
And, at the laughing Galleries Expence,
In secret boast their Cunning and their Sense;
Pretending Things that never can appear
Only at *English Ignorance* to sneer.

If by a smart Return, the Jest to raise,
And throw it on the Laughers, merits Praise;
The *Bottle* justly then your *Plaudit* claim'd.
For that let not this *second* Feint be sham'd.
Since oft You've seen his whole collected Mass,
Dissolv'd, into th'inspiring Vessel pass;
If he again appears, where cou'd he more
Cause your Diversion, or exert his Pow'r?
The Bottle doth some coming Joy denote,
And what can better take it than the Throat?'

VIVITUR
INGENIO

10. Worcester porcelain mug with a transfer-printed scene from a pantomime with Columbine, Harlequin and Pierrot. It dates from 1760–65.

9. 'Shakespeare, Rowe, Johnson, now are quite undone,
These are thy triumphs, thy exploits O Lun!'
A satirical engraving by G. Van der Gucht. Illustration to *Theophilus Cibber, to David Garrick, Esq., with Dissertations on Theatrical Subjects*. Published in 1759. The print shows Rich (Lun) waving *Harlequin Horace; or, The Art of Modern Poetry*, a survey of the degenerate tastes of the day for pantomime and opera (published in 1731) accompanied by Pierrot and Punch driving Poetry (Horace) from the stage of Covent Garden Theatre.

11. *Harlequin Sheppard*. The opening scene in Newgate of John Thurmond's pantomime at Drury Lane Theatre, 1724. A topical pantomime on Jack Sheppard of which *The Weekly Journal or Saturday's Post*, 5 December 1724, said:

'(It) was dismissed with a universal hiss. And, indeed, if Sheppard had been as wretched, and as silly a Rogue in the World, as the ingenious and witty Managers have made him upon the Stage, the lower Gentry, who attended him to Tyburn, wou'd never have pittied him when he was hang'd.' The actor who played Harlequin is unrecorded.

12. Henry Woodward (1714–1777) as Harlequin, with Columbine. Part of an engraving published at the time of his death.

13. *The Player's Last Refuge; or, The Strollers in Distress.* A satirical print. In March 1735 Sir John Barnard moved in the House of Commons for leave to bring in a Bill to limit the number of playhouses and restrain the licentiousness of players, which had, it was averred, increased; and though the Bill miscarried at that time, it was about two years after made law.

Harlequin (Rich) is shown not only as helping the Drama (Hannibal–Cibber?) by offering him a mask and pistols but also by bearing the body of Pistol (Cibber) to a waiting grave.

The explanation under the print says:

'(1) a Strolling Hannibal in Distress. (2) the Ghost of Lun, executed at Kingston, with a Halter about his Neck offering him his Masque and Pistols. (3) Despair and Poverty exciting him to receive the same. (4) a strolling Sophonisba who rather than submit to the Power of the Common Council, heroically deprives herself of Life by a Draught of pure Hollands. (5) Hob having no more to do with his Well is Employ'd in Digging a Grave for Pistol. (6) the Corpse of Pistol supported by Hamlet, Sir John Falstaff, Harlequin, Orpheus, &c. (7) Hippesley, a Retailer of Coffee, Fielding, a retailer of wine, chief Mourners. (8) Sir John Barnard, riding in Triumph o'er the ruins of Troy, Punches Opera, the Sausage and Black pudding stalls, &c. Pointing to a Black Cloud which hangs over Goodman's Fields playhouse.'

This print is important for stage costume, etc., of the period and there is a fuller description on page 10.

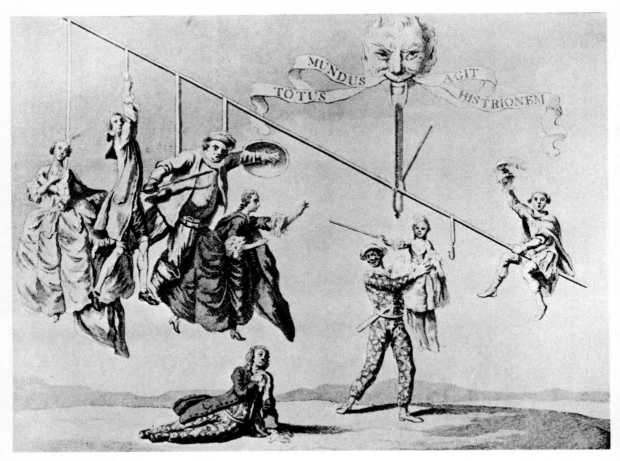

14. 'The Theatrical Steel-Yard of 1750.' This print, published in 1751, satirizes the rivalry of Rich at Covent Garden and David Garrick at Drury Lane. It has been described:–

'At one end of the steel-yard is Garrick waving his helmet triumphantly, and weighing down the united performers at Covent Garden Theatre, not wanting the additional weight of Queen Mab (the pantomime at Drury Lane) whom Woodward, as Harlequin, is ready to place on the hook prepared for her. On the other side, rising, are Peg Woffington, Spranger Barry, James Quin as Falstaff, and Mrs Cibber. On the ground, in great distress, is Rich, with an ample coat thrown over his harlequin dress, grieved to see Garrick alone more attractive at Drury Lane Theatre than those actors who appeared at his own theatre. He was also grieved to find in Woodward his pupil so formidable a rival as a harlequin, in which character he had attained reputation.'

p. 66

15, 16, 17. *Harlequin's Invasion; or, A Christmas Gambol* by David Garrick. First produced at Drury Lane Theatre, 1759. It was revived many times during his management of the theatre, with revision and alterations. John Moody created the part of Simon, and Jane Pope first appeared as Dolly Snip in 1768. Harlequin was created by Thomas King and he was the first to speak in this character.

By His MAJESTY's COMPANY,
At the Theatre Royal, in Drury-Lane,
This present TUESDAY, Dec. 26. 1786.
GEORGE BARNWELL.
George Barnwell by Mr. BANNISTER, Jun.
Trueman by Mr. BARRYMORE,
Thorowgood by Mr. PACKER,
Uncle by Mr. CHAPLIN,
Blunt by Mr. BURTON,
Maria by Mrs. BRERETON,
Lucy by Mrs. WILSON,
And Millwood by Mrs. WARD.
In Act I. a Song by Mr. WILLIAMES,
To which will be added (not acted these Five Years)
the Pantomime Entertainment of

Harlequin's Invasion.
With ALTERATIONS, and RESTORATIONS, particularly the admired
Shades and Transparencies,
Representing the Amusements of HARLEQUIN, and the
Destruction of the PANTOMIMICAL FLEET.
Harlequin by Mr. BANNISTER Jun.
Simon by Mr MOODY,
Gasconade by Mr. BADDELEY,
Mercury by Mr. DIGNUM,
Corporal Bounce by Mr. R. PALMER,
Abram by Mr. WALDRON,
Justice by Mr. CHAPLIN, Forge by Mr. BURTON,
Bogg by Mr PHILLIMORE, Taffy by Mr. WILSON,
Old Woman by Mr. FAWCETT,
And Snip by Mr. SUETT,
Mrs. Snip by Mrs. HOPKINS,
Sukey Chitterlin by Miss COLLINS,
And Dolly Snip by Miss POPE.
To-morrow, Shakespeare's TEMPEST.

18. A pantomime at Covent Garden Theatre *c. 1770*. The print appears to have been first reproduced in this cut version in *Polly Peachum*, by Charles E. Pearce (1913) as from the A. M. Broadley Collection. It was used in Wilson Disher's *Clowns and Pantomimes* (1925) acknowledging the same book. The original print is not to be found in the Broadley Collection now in the Westminster Public Library. As yet this original or a complete print has not been traced.

19. Benefit Ticket for a pantomime, 1787.

20. *Above left.* Lee Lewis (1740–1803) as Harlequin. A Sadler and Green, Liverpool, transfer-printed tile, made in the late 1770s from a contemporary engraving.

21. *Above.* Lee Lewis 'Speaking a prologue in the character of Harlequin'.
   'And shall I mix in this unhallow'd crew?
   May Rosin's lightning blast me if I do.'
Frontispiece to an untraced pantomime book published in 1780. Probably *The Mirror; or, Harlequin Everywhere*, in which he played at Covent Garden Theatre in 1779.

22. *Left.* Benefit Ticket for Sadler's Wells. Late eighteenth-century.

23. *The Mirror; or, Harlequin Everywhere*, by Charles Dibdin. Covent Garden Theatre, 1779.
The opening scene, 'A view of Tartarus, as described in the Pantheon, exhibiting the punishments of Sisyphus, Tantalus, Ixion, Titius, Phleggas, etc.'
Designed and painted by John Inigo Richards.

24. *The Magic Cavern; or, Virtue's Triumph*, by Ralph Wewitzer. Covent Garden Theatre, 1784.
The opening scene, designed and painted by John Inigo Richards.

25. *Top.* Carlo Delpini (1740–1828) as Pierrot (Robinson Crusoe) 'Shooting at the Spaniard' in *Robinson Crusoe; or, Harlequin Friday*, by Richard Sheridan. Drury Lane Theatre, 1781. Delpini was responsible for a change of emphasis in pantomime. Harlequin lost his leading position and Pierrot became the principal character which was to develop into Clown by the turn of the century.

The elder Grimaldi played Friday in this pantomime.

26. *Top right.* Delpini as Pierrot pretending to weep for the death of his master' in *Aladdin; or, The Wonderful Lamp*, by John O'Keefe. Covent Garden Theatre, 1788. Delpini cut the Openings of his pantomimes to a minimum, just introducing the characters and incidents of the story. The rest was 'common racing, hiding, seeking and stealing'.

27. *Right.* Cream-Ware plate transfer-printed with a scene from pantomime.
'The Lovers Parted.
Fair Columbine thy prayers are vain,
For Harlequin and thou must part
Stern Pierrot's leve thou can't obtain,
To join the partner of thy heart.'

The Harlequin wears the new costume devised by James Byrne (1756?–1845). This is probably a scene from *Harlequin Amulet; or, The Magic of Mona*, Drury Lane Theatre, 1800, in which he dressed in 'a white silk shape, fitting without a wrinkle, and into which the variegated silk patches were woven being profusely covered with spangles'.

The Sub-marine Pavilion. — Mother Goose, uniting Harlequin and Columbine.

Mother Goose liberated by Colin.

THEATRE ROYAL, COVENT GARDEN,
This present MONDAY, December 29, 1806,
Will be acted (first time this season) a Tragedy, called

GEORGE BARNWELL;

Or, The LONDON MERCHANT.

Thoroughgood by Mr. MURRAY,   Uncle by Mr. DAVENPORT,
George Barnwell by Mr. C. KEMBLE,
Trueman by Mr. CLAREMONT,   Blunt by Mr. BEVERLY,
Jailer by Mr. ABBOT,   John by Mr. W. Murray,   Robert by Mr. Sarjant,
Officers, Meff. Brown, Platt, Powers,
Maria by Miss BRUNTON,
Millwood by Miss SMITH,
(Being her first appearance in that character.)
Lucy by Mrs. MATTOCKS.

To which will be added, for the first time, a new Pantomime, which has been long in preparation, called

Harlequin and Mother Goose;

OR,

The GOLDEN EGG.

The Scenes, Mufick, Machinery, Dreffes and Decorations are entirely new.

The Overture and Mufick composed by Mr. Ware.
The Pantomime produced under the Direction of Mr. FARLEY—The Dances by Mr. BOLOGNA, Jun.
The SCENERY by Meff. Phillips, Whitmore, Hollogan, Grieve, Hodgins, and their Affiftants
Principal Characters.
Mother Goose, Mr. SIMMONS,
Colin, afterwards Harlequin, by Mr. KING and Mr. BOLOGNA, Jun.
Avaro, afterwards Pantaloon, Mr. L. BOLOGNA,
'Squire Bugle, afterwards Clown, Mr. GRIMALDI,
Beadle, Mr. Denman,   Landlord, Mr. Bologna,   Woodcutter, Mr. Truman,
Cabin-boy (with a Song) Master SMALLEY,   Sergeant, Mr. Banks
Gardeners, Meff. Davis, Dick, Morelli,   Waiters, Meff. Baker & Griffiths
Oddfish, Mr. MENAGE.
Villagers, &c. by Meff. Abbot, T. Blanchard, Brown, Burden, Everard, Fairbrother, Fairclough
Goodwin, Lee, Linton, Meyers, Monk, Odwell, W. Murray, Platt, Powers,
Reeves, Rimsdyck, Sarjant, Street, Tett, J.Tett, Thomas, Wilde.
Fairies, Masters Benton, Goodwin, Morelli, Searle.
Columbine, Miss SEARLE,
Woodcutter's Wife, Mrs. WHITMORE.
Villagers, Fairies, &c. Mesdames Benton, Bologna, L. Bologna, Briftow, Cox, Cranfield, Findlay, Follett
Grimaldi, Iliff, Lefevre, Masters, Price, Slader, Watts.
In the course of the Pantomime (among others) the following NEW SCENERY will be introduced:

VILLAGE, with STORM and SUN RISE.	Hollogan	FLOWER GARDEN.		Grieve
MOTHER GOOSE's HABITATION.	Phillips	St. DUNSTAN's CHURCH		Whitmore
HALL in AVARO's HOUSE.	Hollogan	Entrance of VAUXHALL GARDENS.		Whitmore
COUNTRY INN.	Phillips	Interior of Ditto.		Whitmore
INSIDE of Ditto.	Phillips	GROCER's SHOP, Outfide.		Hollogan
MARKET TOWN.	Phillips	GROCER's PARLOUR.		Phillips
WOODCUTTER's COTTAGE.	Grieve	MERMAID's CAVE.		Whitmore
PAVILION by MOONLIGHT.	Grieve	SUB-MARINE PAVILION.		Hollogan

The Machinery by Meff. SLOPER, BOLOGNA, Jun. CRESWELL, and GOOSTREE.
The Dreffes by Mr. DICK and Mrs. EGAN.
Books of the Songs to be had in the Theatre, Price 9d.   No money to be returned.
Printed by J. Barker, Great Ruffell, 2, Bow-ftreet.   Vivant Rex & Regina.

To-morrow (11th time) the new Play of
ADRIAN and ORRILA; or, A MOTHER's VENGEANCE.
The ninth night of The TEMPEST; or, the ENCHANTED ISLAND, will be on Wednesday

The Gift to her Deliverer.

Entrance of Vauxhall Gardens.

Interior of Vauxhall.

Mother Goose casting the Egg into the Sea.

Mother Goose, raising Spirits, to recover the Egg.

Surprised at the Odd appearance of each other.

Mermaid's Cave, with the recovery of the Egg.

28. *Harlequin and Mother Goose; or, The Golden Egg.* Covent Garden Theatre, 1806. Playbill of the first performance surrounded by a child's writing sheet with scenes from the pantomime.

29. Samuel Simmons as Mother Goose, the Benevolent Agent.

30. Joseph Grimaldi (1779–1837) in *Mother Goose*. 'Sir, I'll just trouble you with a Line.'

31. Grimaldi with John Bologna as Harlequin disguised in 'The favourite Comic Dance' in *Mother Goose*. This pantomime, the work of Charles Dibdin as writer, Charles Farley as producer and with the music of William Ware, combined with the genius of Grimaldi, established the character of Clown as the centre of pantomime for the next fifty years.

32. Thomas Ellar the most famous Harlequin of the Grimaldi era, in 'Positions' and with 'Tricks'. A West juvenile drama sheet, 1812.

33. *Top.* Mrs John Parker as Columbine in *Harlequin and Padmanaba; or, The Golden Fish.* Covent Garden Theatre, 1811. A typical dancer-columbine of the period, from a West juvenile drama sheet.

34. *Top right.* Thomas Blanchard as Pantaloon. A Hodgson Theatrical portrait, 1822.

35. *Right.* Dandy from a juvenile drama sheet *c.* 1830. A Harlequinade character used to satirize the follies of male fashion from the Macaroni of the 1780s to the Heavy Swell of the 1870s.

36. The Royal Circus (later the Surrey Theatre), St George's Circus, Lambeth. An aquatint after Rowlandson and Pugin from *The Microcosm of London*, dated 1809.
The pantomime is possibly *Momus and Mercury: or, Harlequin Hey-Day*, scene 'Thatched House Tavern and New Hotel', produced in 1806 when the theatre reopened.

37. Sadler's Wells Theatre, Islington. An aquatint after Rowlandson and Pugin dated 1809. The final scene, with Neptune's chariot rising from the sea, of an Aquatic Pantomime which cannot so far be identified with certainty.

38. The Little Theatre, Haymarket, 1814. The Dark opening scene, painted by Lupino, of the pantomime *Doctor Hocus-Pocus; or, Harlequin Washed White*, by George Coleman. An old-fashioned pantomime in a new era, but with three Harlequins!

39. Two Clowns from a West juvenile drama sheet of 1812 with the 'traditional' sausages and red hot poker.

40. *Jack and Jill; or, The Clown's Disasters.* Lyceum Theatre, 1812. The Drury Lane Company occupied the theatre while their own was being rebuilt.

41. *Harlequin and Fancy; or, The Poet's Last Shilling.* Drury Lane Theatre, 1815. The transformation scene of the Poet's garret 'rather littered than literary, into a grand museum and menagerie of Fancy filled with all manner of articles animate and inanimate'.

42. *Harlequin Munchausen; or, The Fountain of Love.* Covent Garden Theatre, 1818. The opening scene, a transparency by Thomas Grieve,

'View of mountains of snow near Mount Etna, the burning lava of which gradually melts the snow, and discovers a village which had before lain concealed. Baron Munchausen is seen stretched asleep on the ground, and his horse hanging on the steeple of the village church, to which he had been tied by his master, and where the subsiding snows had left him. The villagers who pass that way express their surprise at so singular an object, but are more astonished when the Baron by cleaving the bridle with a pistol shot brings his horse down in safety, and rides away.'

43. Inside the Inn. 'Comic scene in *Mother Goose*' from a West theatrical sheet, 1812. The ascent and descent of 'magic' chair and table at the touch of Harlequin's wand.

44 and 45. Juvenile drama sheets by West, 1816 and 1827, of pantomime 'tricks' as used in stage productions. Clown turns into a plum pudding or a printing press; Pantaloon into a vase of flowers; a cat into a bag of gold; always at the touch of Harlequin's wand.

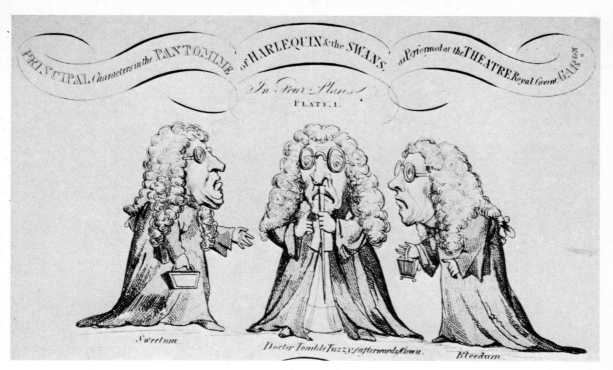

46. *Harlequin and the Swans; or, The Bath of Beauty.* Covent Garden Theatre, 1813. Grimaldi as Doctor Tomble Tuzzy (chief court physician) afterwards Clown, between Sweatum and Bleedum, his assistants disguised in the opening of the pantomime with 'Big Heads' before transformation (once again by Harlequin's wand) into the stock characters.

47. Charles Parslow as Glow Glimmer, the Fire Goblin, and Miss Worgman as Winifreda. After Evil had defied Good, the Fairy enters in her swan-drawn chariot eventually to put matters right.

48. *Harlequin and Asmodeus; or, Cupid on Crutches.* Covent Garden Theatre, 1810. Grimaldi 'Setting to with a Grotesque Figure which he makes up of a series of Vegetables, Fruit &c. and which becoming Animated beats him off the Stage.'

49. *Harlequin and the Red Dwarf; or, The Adamant Rock.* Covent Garden Theatre, 1812. 'Grimaldi's bold Dragoon', a burlesque of the Hussar uniform, with Richard Norman as Pantaloon.

50. *Harlequin and the Red Dwarf.*
'Grimaldi and the Nondescript'. 'The Clown kills the Pantaloon and afterwards Dresses him in the Skin of a Lion, the Head of an Ass, Eagle's Wings, Cat's feet & a Fish's tail.'

51. *Harlequin and the Swans; or, The Bath of Beauty.* Covent Garden Theatre, 1813. Grimaldi's charger. 'A dance, or rather a march, on beer barrels placed on cans, (a very *strong* force) led on by Grimaldi mounted on a charger of a piece with his army, being made up of a barrel laid on a stand, with a funnel for its tail and a hand-saw for its head, caused much laughter.'

52, 53, 54 and 55. West's characters and scenes from *The White Cat; or, Harlequin in the Fairy Wood.* Lyceum Theatre, 1811.

THE WHITE CAT
or
HARLEQUIN in FAIRY WOOD.
— PL. 2nd —

Price 1d Plain.

The Bull in a China Shop

Scene the 9th

SIR TOBY TOUCHY. (afterwards Pantaloon.)

PANTALOON Mr Barnes.

Published as the Act Directs
Jany 8th 1825. by
W. WEST
At his Theatrical Print Warehouse
No 57, Wych Street. Strand.
— LONDON. —

Egyptian Chamber & Museum.

Scene the 5th

DIONYSIUS DAZZLE Esqr (the Rejected Lover.)

LOVER. Mr Hope.

THE WHITE CAT
or
HARLEQUIN
In Fairy Wood
Pl..3.ᵈ

Price 1.ᵈ   Plain.

CHINESE STATUE *(afterwards Clown.)*

Clown & Boy.

CLOWN. Mᵣ Kirby.

Published
as the Act Directs.
Janᵞ 25.ᵗʰ 1825. by
W. WEST.
At his Theatrical Print Warehouse
Nᵒ 57, Wych Street.
~ Strand ~

The Horse Guards.

Scene the 7.ᵗʰ

BURLESQUE HUSSAR OFFICER Mᵣ Buxton.

COLUMBINE Mⁱˢ Valancey.

THE WHITE CAT or HARLEQUIN in FAIRY WOOD.

PL. 4th

Price 1d. Plain.

VAUXHALL BRIDGE

Scene the 11th

TAMBOURINE DANCER *Miss C. Bristow*.

The Clown & Ghost.

DANCER *Mr. Matthews*.

Scene the 10th

Published.
as the Act Directs, Feby. 1. 1825.
by W. WEST. at his
Theatrical Print Warehouse.
57. Wych Street.
Strand.

THE CLOWN *as Huzzar Officer*.

MISS ABIGAIL ANTIQUE *Mr. Chatterley*.

56. *Harlequin and Padmanaba; or, The Golden Fish*. Cove[nt] Garden Theatre, 1811. 'Prime Bang Up.' Grimaldi 'mak[es] a complete Carriage with the following Articles, a Crad[le] four Cheeses, a Green Fender, two Paper Lamps, Blank[ets] for a Great Coat, and a Sheet of Garters for a Whip, &[c.] &c.' A pantomime trick which, in various versions w[as] popular in several pantomimes, satirizing the fashiona[ble] 'four in hand' mania.

57. *Left. Harlequin Harper; or, A Jump from Japan*. Dr[ury] Lane Theatre, 1813. 'The Bristol Dog, Tiger, who [per]forms a variety of astonishing feats and understands [the] language of his master whose commands are given as [to] a person of intellectual capacity and are promptly obey[ed].' The *Theatrical Inquisitor* said:

'In the course of the piece a dog was introduced, w[hich] evinced great docility, and an extraordinary prompti[tude] in understanding and obeying its master's orders.'

58. *Harlequin Whittington, Lord Mayor of London.*
Covent Garden Theatre, 1814. Grimaldi sings
'All the World's in Paris'. Clown satirizing the
craze for fashionable English visitors to go to
France during the brief peace before the Battle
of Waterloo. In the Opening of this pantomime
Grimaldi played Dame Cicely Suet.

59. *Right.* Redigé Paulo as Clown, one of
Grimaldi's chief rivals both at Sadler's Wells
(1817) and at other London theatres. He died in
1835.

Last Night but One of the Company's performing this Season:

Theatre Royal, Drury Lane.

Mr. GRIMALDI'S
BENEFIT,
And LAST APPEARANCE in Public
This Evening. FRIDAY, JUNE 27, 1828.

His Majesty's Servants will commence the Entertainments with the Comic Piece, called

Jonathan in England.

Jonathan W. Doubikins, (a real Yankee, landed at Liverpool) Mr. MATHEWS,
(Who has most liberally tendered his services)
Sir Leatherlip Grossfeeder, Mr. BARTLEY, (his 1st appearance here these two years)
Mr. Ledger, (a Liverpool Merchant) Mr. W. BENNETT,
Mr. Delapierre, (an American Gentleman) Mr. BLAND,
Natty Larkspur, Mr. KEELEY, (his 1st appearance at this Theatre)
Jemmy Larkspur, Mr. TAYLEURE, Tidy, (Waiter at Waterloo Hotel) Mr. SALTER.
Butler to Sir Leatherlip, Mr. MINTON, Agamemnon, (Jonathan's Nigger) Mr. WEBSTER.
Lady Grossfeeder, Mrs. C. JONES, Mary, (her Niece) Miss WESTON.
Patty, Miss NICOL. Mrs. Lemon, Mrs. FIELD; Blanch, (a black Housemaid) Miss GOULD,

After which, the Musical Entertainment of the

ADOPTED CHILD.

Michael,....Mr. WALLACK.
Record, Mr. J. RUSSELL, Le Sage, Mr. BEDFORD, Boy, Miss VINCENT,
Lucy, (1st time) Miss LOVE. in which Character she will sing,
" The Light Guitar," and " I'd be a Butterfly."

To which will be added,

A MUSICAL MELANGE.

"Se D'Amor fra le Ritorte."..[Paccini]....by Madame FERON.
Song—" Bundle of Conundrums"....by Mr. KEELEY.
Song—" Oh no, we never mention her."........Miss LOVE.
Song—" The Almanack Maker,"............by Mr. HARLEY.
"La Biondina in Gondoletta".....by Miss FANNY AYTON.
Song—" Don't say Nay!" by Mr. MORGAN, the celebrated Irish Vocalist.

In the course of the Evening will be exhibited the splendid Panoramic View of The

BATTLE of WATERLOO

Painted by STANFIELD.—During which will be performed
Weber's celebrated Overture to " Kampf und Sieg."
With the revived Extravaganza, called

Harlequin Hoax.

Persons without Characters——Stage Manager, Mr. THOMPSON, Patch, (the Author) Mr. J. RUSSELL.
Prompter, Mr. FENTON, Factotum, Mr. HONNOR, Call Boy, Mr. RICHARDSON.
Persons with Characters, proposed for the intended Pantomime——Syrens, Miss GOULD and Miss WILLMOTT.
Harlequin......Mr. HARLEY.
Columbine....Miss KELLY, (her 1st appearance here this season)
The whole to conclude with a SELECTION of POPULAR SCENES from the most approved and successful

COMIC PANTOMIMES.

INTERIOR of BARBER's SHOP, from the Pantomime of THE MAGIC FIRE.
Clown........Mr. GRIMALDI,
As originally performed by him—in which he will introduce his favourite Song of
" HOT CODLINGS."
A favourite Scene from HARLEQUIN IN HIS ELEMENT.
Clown, Mr. J. S. GRIMALDI (from the Theatre Royal Covent Garden.)
Public House and Gambling House, from the BABES in the WOOD.
Harlequin, Mr. HOWELL, Pantaloon Mr. BARNES, Clown, Mr. SOUTHBY. Columbine, Miss RYAL.
A popular Scene from Mother Bunch.
Harlequin, Mr. RIDGWAY, Pantaloon, Mr. J. RIDGWAY. Clown. Mr. T. RIDGWAY.
COMIC PAS DE DEUX, by Master WIELAND and Master CHIKINI.
In the Last Scene....A brilliant Display of Fire-Works.
Previous to which, Mr. GRIMALDI will deliver his
FAREWELL ADDRESS.

To-morrow, Town and Country. Cosey, Mr. Dowton.
Reuben Glenroy, Mr. Wallack. Rosalie Somers, Miss Lawrence. With The RIVAL SOLDIERS.
Nipperkin. Mr. Mathews. Mary, Miss Love. After which, A MUSICAL MELANGE.
To conclude with KATHERINE and PETRUCHIO. Petruchio. Mr. Wallack.
Katherine, Miss Lawrence. For the Benefit of Mr. SPRING.
And the Last Night of the Company's performing this Season.
VIVAT REX. J. Tabby, Printer, Theatre Royal, Drury Lane.

60 and 61. Grimaldi's Farewell, Drury Lane Theatre, 27 June 1828. Playbill and drawing made there by H. Brown, who was a member of the orchestra at Sadler's Wells Theatre. After his last performance Grimaldi delivered a farewell address written for him by Tom Hood:

'Ladies and Gentlemen, I appear before you for the last time. I need not assure you of the sad regret with which I say it; but sickness and infirmity have come upon me, and I can no longer wear the motley! Four years ago I jumped my last jump, filched my last custard, and ate my last sausage. I cannot describe the pleasure I felt on once more assuming my cap and bells tonight—that dress in which I have so often been made happy in your applause; and as I stripped them off, I fancied that they seemed to cleave to me. I am not so rich a man as I was when I was basking in your favour formerly, for then I had always a fowl in one pocket and sauce for it in the other. (Laughter and applause from the audience.) I thank you for the benevolence which has brought you here to assist your old and faithful servant in his premature decline. Eight-and-forty years have not yet passed over my head, and I am sinking fast. I now stand worse on my legs than I used to do on my head. But I suppose I am paying the penalty of the cause I pursued all my life; my desire and anxiety to merit your favour has excited me to more exertion than my con-stitution would bear, and, like vaulting ambition, I have overleaped myself. Ladies and Gentlemen, I must hasten to bid you farewell; but the pain I feel in doing so is assuaged by see-ing before me a disproof of the old adage that favourites have no friends. Ladies and Gentlemen, may you and yours ever enjoy the blessings of health is the fervent prayer of Joseph Grimaldi—Farewell! Farewell!'

62. Grimaldi, Tom Ellar and James Barnes. A watercolour by H. Brown *c.* 1825.

63. *Puss in Boots: or, Harlequin and the Miller's Son.* Covent Garden Theatre, 1832. Elizabeth Poole as Josselin (the Miller's son), William Mitchenson as Tibbytight and Mary Horton as Goody Greylocks, (Cat-a-Rosa, assistant to Felina the Protector of the Feline Race, in disguise).

64. Elizabeth Poole and William Mitchenson in *Puss in Boots.* The finale in 'The Silver Temple, or Felina's Palace', from a painting by Henry Meyer in the Garrick Club. In this pantomime, by Charles Farley, there were two Clowns, Paulo being 'Clown to Harlequin' and Tom Matthews 'Clown to Pantaloon'. William Mitchenson, (a pupil of Matthews') later to play Sprites and Goblins until he grew up, remained a dancer and pantomimist, as well as an actor, at the London and Minor theatres until he died in 1870 at the age of 49.

65. Tom Matthews (1805–1899) as Clown. From a lithograph by John Brandard. He was considered the successor to Grimaldi and had to sing his predecessor's songs. He appeared at Covent Garden, Drury Lane and Sadler's Wells until the 1850s, the last of the traditional Clowns as the part dwindled away.

HERE WE ARE AGAIN

A SCENE FROM THE PANTOMIME AT THE ADELPHI.

A SCENE FROM THE PANTOMIME AT SADLER'S WELLS—"ROBIN HOOD AND FRIAR TUCK"

A SCENE FROM THE PANTOMIME AT COVENT GARDEN—"A LECTURE ON SOAP SUDS."

A SCENE FROM THE PANTOMIME AT ASTLEY'S—"JOHN GILPIN'S RIDE."

A SCENE FROM THE PANTOMIME AT THE SURREY—"KING SOVEREIGN'S SURPRISE.

67. *King Jamie; or, Harlequin and The Magic Fiddle.* Princess's Theatre, 1849. The royal bedroom with the baby Prince Charles keeping his parents awake. An historical plot for an Opening by G. H. Rodwell: 'Here, in the Hall of Evil Spirits, we are introduced to Alcohol, exiled by Father Mathew, and the Water Cure, who conspires against the peace of King James, ending his many plots with the Gunpowder Plot. Guy Faux and his party are frightened away by Old Seymour, the Scotch blind fiddler, who escapes with his Royal companion. The opening of Parliament then succeeds; the fun consisting in representing the statesmen of the present day in grotesque masks. After a few more palpable hits of a similar kind, the changes occur.'

The acting company (in Big Heads) were completely separated from the Harlequinade characters. The Drury Lane pantomime this year was based on the story of Queen Elizabeth and the Earl of Leicester.

66. *Opposite.* The pantomimes of Christmas 1844. *Cat's Castle; or, Harlequin and the King of the Rats*, Adelphi Theatre. *Harlequin Robin Hood and Little John; or, 'Merrie England' in the Olden Time*, Sadler's Wells. *Harlequin Crotchet and Quaver; or, Music for the Million*, Covent Garden Theatre. *Harlequin and Johnny Gilpin's Ride; or, The Black Witch of Edmonton*, Astley's Amphitheatre. *Pounds, Shillings and Pence; or, Harlequin £.S.D.*, Surrey Theatre.

68. *Harlequin Yankee Doodle came to Town upon his Little Pony!* 'A transatlantic and Britannic' Equestrian Pantomime by Nelson Lee. Astley's Amphitheatre, 1849. The Transformation scene 'Britannia's Coral Cave'. 'At this moment the entire scene changes: Britannia appears and settles the dispute for the present, by changing Yankee Doodle to Clown, England to Harlequin, Old Sambo to Pantaloon, and Miss Dinah to Columbine. Then follows the Harlequinade, with hits at past and passing events, &c.'

69. The Harlequinade characters on horseback as transformed by Britannia. Columbine, Louisa Davidson; Harlequin, W. H. Harvey; Clown, Mr Jackson and Pantaloon, Mr Craddock.

70. *Harlequin Baron Munchausen and his Comical Cream Cob Cruizer; or, The Queen of the Fairy Steed's Haunt.* Astley's Amphitheatre, 1858. 'The transformation-tableau at Astley's, in accordance with the traditions and objects of the cirque, combines equestrian with pictorial and mechanical effects. The scene in which the pantomime change takes place— "The Golden Bird's Home"—is one of great beauty and brilliancy; and the introduction of magnificent fairy chariots drawn by pigmy steeds, and equestrian female figures picturesquely disposed through the scene, adds greatly to the beauty of the whole.'

71. Richard Flexmore (1824–1860), Clown and dancer at the principal London theatres. 'He was especially noted for his close and natural imitations of the leading dancers of the day', particularly the many Spanish dancers who visited London in the 1850s.

72. *King Humming Top; or, Harlequin and the Land of Toys.*
Drury Lane Theatre, 1853. 'The Hall of Christmas Revels.'

73. *Romeo and Juliet; or, Harlequin Queen Mab and the World of Dreams.* Olympic Theatre, 1852. Shakespeare made into an Opening where 'The apothecary sells Romeo a bottle of British brandy. There is no antidote for such a poison, as poor Romeo finds; and Juliet stabs herself at the moment when the Friar and Old Capulet make their appearance. The tomb bursting open to the Halls of Refulgent Light, discovers Queen Mab in her chair of state, and the transformations take place.'

74. *Jack and the Beanstalk; or, Harlequin and Mother Goose at Home Again.* Adelphi Theatre, 1855. 'A Grand Coalition of Burlesque and Comic Pantomime.' Madame Celeste and Miss Wyndham as Harlequin and Columbine *à la Watteau.* It was remarked that 'when Actors and Actresses not pantomimists condescend to such characters as Clown and Pantaloon and Harlequin and Columbine have Madame Celeste herself and Miss Wyndham for their representatives, it will be readily conceived that not alone a mere material vehicle of whim has been provided, but that the whole is realised and animated by intellectual capacity of high histrionic rank.' And Pantomime has a 'Principal Boy'.

75. *Aladdin and the Wonderful Lamp; or, Harlequin and the Genie of the Ring.* Princess's Theatre, 1856. A John Maddison Morton pantomime, under Charles Kean's management. 'A Winter's Tale—St James's Park.' La Zartoriski Polka danced by Harlequin, John Cormack, and Columbine, Caroline Adams.

76. *Little Red Riding Hood; or, Harlequin and the Wolf in Grannie's Clothing.* Royal Opera House, Covent Garden, 1858. The first pantomime in the new Opera House, described as a 'new little pantomime for little people'. Grannie's cottage bedroom is on operatic scale.

77. *The King of the Castle; or, Harlequin Prince Diamond and Princess Brighteyes.* Princess's Theatre, 1858. Pantaloon, James Paulo; Columbine, Caroline Adams; Harlequin, John Cormack; Clown junior, James Huline Jr and Clown, James Huline.

78. *Ye Belle Alliance; or, Harlequin Good Humour and Ye Fielde of Ye Clothe of Golde.* Covent Garden, 1855. A pantomime which included a double Harlequinade and a patriotic spectacle to celebrate the ending of the Crimean War. 'The concluding scene, "The Apotheosis of ye Belle Alliance", designed by M. Guérin, is a masterpiece of scenic design and structural contrivance. In the midst are mourners at the tomb of the slain; on either side groups of soldiers, representing every regiment in the English, French and Sardinian army; and above, the victors, enthroned and crowned with coronals of valour by the Genius of Victory, who descends from the skies to complete the tableau.'

79. 'Pantorama of the Pantomime', a children's picture book, published by S. Marks and Son, *c.* 1860. The eight scenes are the essence of Victorian pantomime. From the 'Big Head' opening fairy story.

80. The intervention of the Good Fairy at the moment of crisis, and the Prince becomes Harlequin.

81. The Good Fairy gives Harlequin his magic bat and he transforms the cast into the traditional characters.

82. Tricks and acrobatics.

83. Fun at the expense of contemporary fashion.

84. The topical joke. Clown and Pantaloon as rival omnibus drivers fight for the custom of the Dandy, interrupted by the inevitable Policeman.

85. The Chase. Clown and Pantaloon steal clothes and are pursued by the Tailor.

86. The Finale and all comes right in the end.

87. *Puss in Boots; or, Harlequin and the Fairy of the Golden Palms.* Covent Garden, 1859. 'The court of Queen Innocentia', Queen of the good fairies, where later she reviews her subjects who have all enlisted as rifle volunteers, in consequence of suspicious movements of a certain Worldlinesse, who is a near neighbour.

88. Pantomime Ballet on an open stage at the Crystal Palace, 1864. 'The platform in front of Shakespeare's House has been converted into a stage for the gambols of Harlequins with Columbines and Clowns, or for the dangerous feats of high-flying gymnasts on the trapeze; the graceful evolutions of Jackson Haines, the American Skater; the grotesque contortions of Herr Willio, "the Flexible Gnome"; the rope trick, performed in a closed cupboard or watch-box, by the Brothers Nemo, without any diabolical aid; or the intelligent dog whom Jean Bond has taught to behave like a thinking animal. A pantomimic ballet, composed by Nelson Lee, was the concluding spectacle. The gigantic Clown's head, which overlooks the roof of Shakespeare's dwelling, is a fit president for this occasion.'

89. *Aladdin and the Wonderful Lamp; or, Harlequin and the Flying Palace.* Covent Garden, 1865. 'The Enchanted Cavern in the Garden of Jewels' where Aladdin (Rachel Sanger) finds the lamp, in a setting by Thomas Grieve.

90. *Little King Pippin; or, Harlequin Fortunatus and the Magic Purse and Wishing-cap.* Drury Lane, 1865. 'The induction opens with the Temple of Mammon, the dirty deity himself being rather too majestically represented by Henri Drayton, who supplies Fortune with the inexhaustible purse, which, ultimately, she bestows on Fortunatus. But will the boundless supply of wealth thereby imparted secure happiness for the possessor?' A setting by William Beverley. Both pantomimes at Covent Garden and Drury Lane were by E. L. Blanchard and seemed to harp on the lust for wealth.

91. Engaging children for the Christmas pantomime at Drury Lane Theatre, 1867 (see page 25).

92. 'Preparing for the Pantomime'. Lyceum Theatre, 1868 (see page 25).

93. 'The Children's Pantomime Party' at Covent Garden, 1871, by F. W. Lawson. 'A party, taken to see the Pantomime by a gentleman, a friend of Mamma's. I'm in the picture I know because I saw it before it was printed. I'm the little girl in the left-hand corner, with her hands clutched together.'

94. 'Returning from the Pantomime', Charing Cross Station, 1871, by J. M. L. Ralston. 'Half-past eleven o'clock at night is too late for such little ones to be knocking about in town. For those who live at Sydenham or at Blackheath, and trust to the last railway train, at midnight, for their return to a suburban villa, the necessity of catching a cab and driving fast to Charing Cross station, with a party of tired or excited youngsters, is rather an anxious affair, but they manage somehow to get to the railway station in plenty of time.'

95. 'The First Night of a new Pantomime', 1868. A watercolour by Charles Green in the possession of Osborne Robinson. It is thought that it represents the stage of the Britannia Theatre, Hoxton.

96. 'The "Star Trap" ', Princess's Theatre, 1874, by F. Villiers (see page 27).

98. *Puss in Boots; or, Dame Trot and her Comical Cat and the Ogre, Fee-fo-Fum.* Crystal Palace, 1873. Josselin, Caroline Parkes; the Ogre, George Conquest; Puss, George Conquest Jr. 'The Ogre's castle with its enchanted chamber, in which Mr Conquest performs his hanky-panky tricks, and assumes various shapes, dilating into gigantic proportions, or shrinking into those of the dwarf, and even the mouse, in which latter form he is pounced on by Puss, and his fate determined. The work is produced on the great stage in the centre transept, and the auditorium is crowded with multitudes of spectators, themselves presenting a spectacle scarcely to be rivalled by the most costly arrangements of the boards.'

97. 'The "English Trap"' from *Trucs et Décors* by Georges Moynet, 1893.

Dressmaking

Property Room

Boiling the Size

Mr Beverly's Painting Room

99. 'Preparing for the Pantomime: Notes at Drury Lane', by F. Villiers, 1874 (see page 26).

100. *Blue Beard.* Covent Garden, 1871. By Henry J. Byron, with music by Gilbert H. Betjemann. Procession of Blue Beard (J. H. Macdermott) and his retinue. A lithograph music-front by Alfred Concanen.

101. *Cinderella.* Covent Garden, 1875. W. B. Fair and John Wainwright as the Ugly Sisters, Salprunella and Blowsabella; J. H. Rogers as Baron Blunderboar; Miss Amalia as Cinderella; Maud Brennan as Flunkini and Nellie Power as Plenteous, Prince of Luxuria.

102. *Beauty and the Beast; or, Harlequin and Old Mother Bunch.* Drury Lane, 1869. The Forest of Apes. 'Inhabitants of the Forest by an Extraordinary Troupe of Performing Monkeys', led by the Baboon, William Mitchenson. This pantomime had a double Harlequinade with the addition of a Harlequina for good measure.

103. *Whittington and his Cat; or, Harlequin Lord Mayor of London.* Drury Lane, 1875. The Vokes family. Walter (Fawdon), the Cat; Frederick, Fitzwarren; Victoria, Dick Whittington; Rosina, Alice, and Jessie as the Fairy Bluebell rendering supernatural aid.

104. *Harlequin and the White Cat.* Drury Lane, 1877. 'The scene illustrated is one of palatial proportions, and represents the magnificent appointments of a fairy-tale hunting château, with the talented Vokes family and Harriett Coveney in the leading parts.'

105. *Little Goody Two-Shoes; or, Harlequin Little Boy Blue.* Adelphi Theatre, 1876. 'A Children's Pantomime performed entirely by children.' Pantaloon, Master Meadows; Harlequin, Constance Gilchrist; Clown, Bertie Coote and Columbine, Carrie Coote. Children's performances of pantomime and Gilbert and Sullivan Operas became a fashion at this period and provided a breeding ground for future stars. Harry Grattan, Kate Seymour and Ada Blanche were all in the Adelphi Company which was produced by John Cormack.

106. Harry Nicholls as Haw Haw in *Hokee Pokee, the Fiend of the Fungus Forest; or, The Six Links of the Devil's Chain.* Grecian Theatre, 1878. A topical song 'There's more to follow', sung in a typical pantomime costume by 'a Hong Kong howling swell rejoicing in the name of Haw Haw. The make-up for this character is marvellously droll. The howling swell looks like a mixture of a street acrobat, an undertaker's mute, Mr Micawber waiting for something to turn up.'

107. *Spitz-Spitz the Spider Crab; or, The Pirate of Spitzbergen.* Grecian Theatre, 1875. By George Conquest and Henry Spry. George Conquest as the Ice King disguised as a Monster Crab and a Dwarf, his son, George Jr, as the Fire King, assisted by Lizzie Conquest, Dot Robins and Herbert Campbell. 'The phantom fight scene transcended our experience and cannot be described.'

108. *Turlututa; or, The Three Enchanted Hats.* Britannia Theatre, Hoxton, 1876. Good, in the person of Sara Lane as Phospharielle, defeats *Il Diavolo*, Pollie Randall, who descends in a cloud of red fire.

109. *Robin Hood.* Alexandra Theatre, Liverpool, 1880. Eily Morley as Will Scarlett and Lily Meredith as Maude. 'Though both their parts were remarkably small, and allowed very little scope for either speech or action, still what little these clever young ladies had to say and do, they said and did to perfection.'

110. *Robinson Crusoe*. Drury Lane, 1881. Fannie Leslie as Crusoe in E. L. Blanchard's pantomime:

'Another notch to mark another day
Ah me! unlike this knife time cuts away.'

III. 'Rehearsing for the Pantomime' by A. Forestier. Covent Garden, 1881. *Little Bo-Peep, Little Boy Blue and the Little Old Woman that Lived in a Shoe.* 'Written and produced under the direction of William Young.'

'No greater contrast exists than a theatre lighted up at night, full of well dressed and happy people, the music playing from a full orchestra, and the stage a blaze of brilliancy; and a theatre in the morning, dull, cold and deathlike, gloomy and draughty, the daylight creeping through cracks and crevices, and struggling with the gas, and the artists engaged on a rehearsal as despondent as the scene. Let no one who does not wish to suffer the shame of disillusion venture within a theatre at daytime. In front of the house the darkened passages are possessed by mysterious charwomen, who flit about mournfully, as if in the catacombs. The stranger runs a risk of breaking his neck at every step, and if, more by luck than anything else, he arrives on the stage, he will find the feeling of profound melancholy intensified until it reaches the very note of despair. Yet here, in this uncongenial atmosphere, and on this uncongenial scene, are prepared with minuteness and indefatigable care all the effects that become so dazzling hereafter. Here the dancers, in ordinary walking attire, practise their steps up in a corner; here the comic man, with the melancholy countenance, leans over the orchestra and hums over his screaming song to the conductor, who has the tune played by a solitary fiddle; here the scene-painter and the master carpenter are in an animated discussion over a matter with which the author has nothing whatever to do; here imps and fairies in most modern and Drury Lane attire scamper about, playing hide and seek about the scenery until they arouse the anger of the stage manager; here processions are drilled and pantomime tricks are invented, and the clown goes through his business with pantaloon and harlequin, and the leading young lady says such pretty things to the author and beams at him just to get two or three more lines inserted and an extra verse added to a song already too long. Here those who are not on in every scene lounge aimlessly about and waste a considerable amount of time; still, on the whole, those who are so disposed to abuse the theatres, and to accuse them of encouraging frivolity and what not, would find a vast amount of honest hard work, patience, skill, and good temper in the countless manufactories of pleasure when the human machinery is set going and they are rehearsing for the pantomime.'

112. 'Rehearsing for the Pantomime at Drury Lane Theatre' by A. Forestier, 1882. *Sindbad the Sailor* by E. L. Blanchard. 'The whole invented, arranged and produced under the direction of Augustus Harris.'

'The Drury Lane pantomime will be of a very elaborate character, as neither time, pains, nor money have been spared in its preparation. One of the most striking features will be the procession of English Kings and Queens from William the Norman down to Her Most Gracious Majesty Queen Victoria, who will walk out of the Tower of London with their attendants, and welcome the conquering heroes from Egypt. It might be appropriately called the March of Ages. The Kings and Queens by themselves, would not present such a very imposing array; but they will severally be followed by so many knights, pages, and men-at-arms, that there will be at least 500 persons on the stage at once; and the boards at old Drury have been described as "like a town". There would not have been space enough for this procession, had not the manager bethought him at the eleventh hour that at the back there was a largish building used for the storage of scenery; so the main wall has been pulled down, an archway formed, and the stage extended to exactly double its original dimensions. Every dress in its minutest detail has been studied from old books and drawings in the British Museum; and of such magnificent material and workmanship are some of them that they have cost not less than £35 a piece, and £1000 has been spent on them altogether. At the ordinary rehearsal, of which we give an Illustration, all the performers, ladies and gentlemen, are in their common outdoor dress, instead of their theatrical costumes. As for Mr Harris, his energy is almost incredible, for he marshals each "reign" separately and marches alongside them, stick in hand, till convinced that that particular detachment of his forces is prepared to do its duty. When satisfied with them, he calls for the next "reign," and so on, and so on, till all have gone through the part allotted to them. It is capital policy, for the master's eye does more work than both his hands; and, in this case, the overlooking of the smallest detail might spoil the effect of the whole, and what might occur if any of the following of Farmer George got mixed up with that of Bloody Mary is fearful to contemplate. The "business" of each sovereign is very realistic. King John is surrounded by turbulent Barons, who insist on obtaining his signature to Magna Charta, and Oliver Cromwell is very emphatic in his scorn for the mace. The ladies concerned with Henry VIII form quite an imposing array, and that much-married monarch is the *beau idéal* of Bluff King Hal. Every individual is known to the enterprising lessee and manager by a number; and so clear is his conception of what each one has to do that he instantly detects the slightest variation. Several thousand pounds have been laid out in bringing all the accessories of the procession to perfection.'

(NELLY POWER AS SINDBAD IN DRURY LANE PANTOMIME)

113. Nellie Power as Sindbad the Sailor. Drury Lane, 1882. Drawn by Alfred Chasemore who designed the costume.

'When Sindbad the Sailor first started at sea,
He was just about ill as a fellow could be;
"I wish I was home with my mother" says
   he,
"It's awful" says Sindbad the Sailor.
"Throw me over-board Captain" he cried,
  "I beseech!
I'm ill and this lesson the voyage will teach,
Home isn't the only thing now I shall reach
Where's the steward?" says Sindbad the
   Sailor.

"As a friend of Gus Harris I mean to remain,
So drop in and see me at old Drury Lane,
And in glitter and glory I'll tell you again
The story of Sindbad the Sailor."

114. Vesta Tilley as Captain Tra-la-la (of the Khedives' Own), in *Sindbad the Sailor*. Drury Lane, 1882. The long waits and the length of the performance on Boxing night produced a rowdy audience and *Punch* said:
'The loudly expressed disapprobation warned the music hall Favourites, that, off their own peculiar platform, it was dangerous to presume on their exceptional popularity.'
The evening included a grand procession of 'The Kings and Queens of England' concluding with a review of the British troops back from Egypt.

115. Harry Payne, one of the last traditional Clowns. From 1880, with one or two intervals, he was at Drury Lane each year. He had played Lover in earlier days but, as his obituary in 1895 said, 'Gradually, however, pantomime gave way to the somewhat vulgar burlesque with which we are now familiar, and Payne's art was relegated to the background. He turned Clown, and as such will long be remembered.'

116. Walter Hildyard Todd, Clown at Covent Garden, 1881, and other London and provincial theatres until he retired in 1889. A lithograph by Jules Chéret made during his early days in London. He also designed a Rimmel fan programme for the Gaiety Theatre in 1869.

117. Harry Nicholls and Herbert Campbell as Tom (the Idle Apprentice) and Eliza (the Cook) sing 'D'you think so? Yes, I think so!'. *Whittington and his Cat*. Drury Lane, 1884.

118. Harry Nicholls and Herbert Campbe[ll] the Queen and the King in *Puss in Boots*. D[rury] Lane, 1887. 'Marry come up! Forsooth! Go

119. *Puss in Boots*. Drury Lane, 1887. Charles Lauri as Puss presenting himself to the royal family in a palace scene. Designed and costumed by Charles Wilhelm.

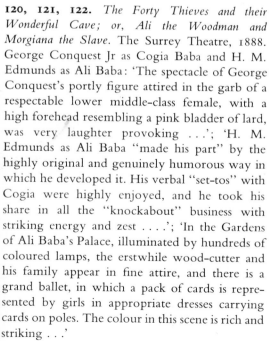

120, 121, 122. *The Forty Thieves and their Wonderful Cave; or, Ali the Woodman and Morgiana the Slave.* The Surrey Theatre, 1888. George Conquest Jr as Cogia Baba and H. M. Edmunds as Ali Baba: 'The spectacle of George Conquest's portly figure attired in the garb of a respectable lower middle-class female, with a high forehead resembling a pink bladder of lard, was very laughter provoking . . .'; 'H. M. Edmunds as Ali Baba "made his part" by the highly original and genuinely humorous way in which he developed it. His verbal "set-tos" with Cogia were highly enjoyed, and he took his share in all the "knockabout" business with striking energy and zest . . . .'; 'In the Gardens of Ali Baba's Palace, illuminated by hundreds of coloured lamps, the erstwhile wood-cutter and his family appear in fine attire, and there is a grand ballet, in which a pack of cards is represented by girls in appropriate dresses carrying cards on poles. The colour in this scene is rich and striking . . .'

123. *Top left.* Costume design by Charles Wilhelm for Clara Thompson as Little Boy Blue in *Little Bo-Peep, Little Boy Blue and the Little Old Woman that Lived in a Shoe*. Covent Garden, 1881.

124. *Above.* Costume designs by Charles Wilhelm: Letty Lind as Princess Sweetarte in *Puss in Boots*. Drury Lane, 1887.

125. *Left.* A Palace Guard in *Puss in Boots*. Drury Lane, 1887.

Opposite
Top left and right
126. A Japanese Lily in 'The Flower Ballet', *Little Bo-Peep*. Covent Garden, 1881.

127. The Fairy Bowbell in *Dick Whittington*. Theatre Royal, Manchester, 1885.

Below left and right
128. A Fairy in *The Sleeping Beauty*, 1886.

129. Miss Mathews as Chanticleer in *Little Red Riding Hood; or, The Wizard and the Wolf*. Her Majesty's Theatre, 1883.

130. *Cinderella*. Lyceum Theatre, 1893. Minnie Terry as the Sylph Coquette.

'Nimble are fingers of fairies at work;
They never tire and their task never shirk.'

131. *Cinderella*. Lyceum Theatre, 1893. Ellalin Terriss as Cinderella.

'Life's path to me seems very rough and steep

132. *Robinson Crusoe*. Lyceum Theatre, 18 The Prologue. Geraldine Somerset as Spirit of Adventure.

''Tis I that make young Britons brave and bo

133. Ada Blanche as Robinson Crusoe. Drury Lane, 1893.

134. Marie Lloyd as Polly Perkins. *Robinson Crusoe*. Drury Lane, 1893.

135. Herbert Campbell and Dan Leno as Eliza the Cook and Idle Jack. *Dick Whittington*. Drury Lane, 1894. Contemporary burlesque of 'The New Woman' and a guardsman.

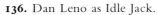

136. Dan Leno as Idle Jack.

137. Dan Leno as the Baroness. *Cinderella.* Drury Lane, 1895.

138. Dan Leno as Mrs Twankey. *Aladdin.* Drury Lane, 1896.

139. Dan Leno and Herbert Campbell as Reggie and Chrissie. *Babes in the Wood.* Drury Lane, 1897.

140. Dan Leno and Herbert Campbell as Abdallah and the Fair Zuleika. *The Forty Thieves.* Drury Lane, 1898.

141. Harriet Vernon as Prince Charming. *Cinderella.*

142. Vesta Tilley as Dick Whittington. Theatre Royal, Newcastle-upon-Tyne, 1893.

143. Marie Lloyd as Little Boy Blue. *Bo-Peep, Little Boy Blue and The Merry Old Woman who Lived in a Shoe.* Shakespeare Theatre, Liverpool, 1894.

144. Billie Barlow as Little Boy Blue. *Red Riding Hood and Little Boy Blue.* Theatre Royal, Birmingham, 1893.

145. Marie Lloyd in *Dick Whittington; or, Harlequin the Fairy Spells and the Talkative Bells.* Crown Theatre, Peckham, 1898.

146. Marie Loftus as Sindbad the Sailor. Theatre Royal, Glasgow, 1896.

147. Vesta Tilley as Robinson Crusoe. Prince's Theatre, Manchester, 1895.

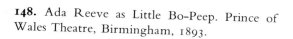

148. Ada Reeve as Little Bo-Peep. Prince of Wales Theatre, Birmingham, 1893.

149. Constance Churton as Apollo in *Jack and the Beanstalk*. Theatre Royal, Manchester, 1895. 'The Man in the Moon greets Jack at the top of the beanstalk, introducing him to the Gods and Goddesses and helping him on his way to the Giant's Castle.'

150. Alexandra Dagmar as Dandini. *Cinderella*. Drury Lane, 1895. The Dandy and excesses of military uniform combined.

151. *Aladdin.* Princes Theatre, Bristol, 1899. The Garden of Aladdin's Palace.
152, 153, 154. Ada Reeve as three Aladdins.
Prince of Wales Theatre, Birmingham, 1892. A daring cigarette for an eighteen year old principal boy. Bristol, 1899. Singing 'The Absent-minded Beggar', a patriotic song by Kipling and Sullivan, at the time of the South African War. Prince of Wales Theatre, Birmingham, 1905. Aladdin eventually becomes a boy of the Peking streets. She last played the part in Australia, in 1924.

155, 156. *Jack and the Beanstalk*. Shakespeare Theatre, Liverpool, 1908. Ada Reeve as Jack.

157, 158. *Cinderella.* Shakespeare Theatre, Liverpool, 1907. Alice Russon, Cinderella, and George Lashwood, Dandini, who sang his popular music hall song 'Put me among the girls' as a Regency rake.

159, 160. *Cinderella*. Shakespeare Theatre Liverpool, 1907. The fairy godmother Marie West, sees Cinderella off to the ball, and Prince Charming, Madoline Rees, arrives with the slipper.

161. Dan Leno as Mother Goose. Drury Lane, 1903.

162. Dan Leno as Mother Goose after a visit to the Magic Pool.

163. Dan Leno as Sister Ann in *Blue Beard*. Drury Lane, 1901.

164. Dan Leno as Queen Spritely in *Humpty Dumpty*. Drury Lane, 1903.

165. Charles Lauri as the Poodle in *Sindbad the Sailor*. Drury Lane, 1888. He played monkeys, cats and dogs at Drury Lane for many years and was famous for his walk round the edge of the circle among the audience in these characters.

166. Arthur Conquest with Priscilla the Cow. *Jack and the Beanstalk*. Drury Lane, 1910. The third generation of the pantomime family who played with the Drury Lane Company each year from 1901 to 1915, returning in 1919 and 1920.

167. Daisy Cordell as the Fairy Godmother. *Cinderella*, Drury Lane, 1905.

168. Alec Davidson as Father Neptune. *Humpty Dumpty*, Drury Lane, 1903.

169. George Bastow as Peter in *Humpty Dumpty*. Drury Lane, 1903. The ever popular 'Schoolroom' scene.

170. Harry Fragson as Dandigny. *Cinderella*. Drury Lane, 1905. An Anglo-French entertainer fitted into English pantomime as a male French Dandini.

171. Harry Randall as Little Mary in *Humpty Dumpty*. Drury Lane, 1903. A second 'Dame' part created during Dan Leno's last illness.

Opposite

172. Florrie Ford, the great music hall chorus singer, who played principal boy in her native Australia before she came to London in 1897. She continued to play the part up to the 1930s.

173. Queenie Leighton as Prince Jasper. *Cinderella*. Drury Lane, 1905.

174. Sybil Arundale as Dick Whittington. Theatre Royal, Birmingham, 1908. Now Lord Mayor of London and resplendent in the 'Walk down' robes.

175. Hetty King as Aladdin. Royal Court Theatre, Liverpool, 1904. The famous male impersonator chose to be a very feminine principal boy.

Opposite

176. George Robey as Dame Trot in *Jack and the Beanstalk*. Theatre Royal, Birmingham, 1909.

177. George Robey as Queen of Hearts. Royal Court Theatre, Liverpool, 1905.

178. Alfred Wellesley as Queen of Hearts in *Jack Horner*. Prince's Theatre, Bristol, 1910.

179. Wilkie Bard as Mother Goose. Prince's Theatre, Bristol, 1905.

Above

180. Phyllis Dare as Cinderella. Theatre Royal, Newcastle-upon-Tyne, 1906.

181. Zena Dare as Princess Beauty in *Beauty and the Beast*. Prince's Theatre, Bristol, 1904.

Right

182. Maidie Andrews and Lupino Lane in *Babes in the Wood*. Shakespeare Theatre, Liverpool, 1905.

183. Dorothy Ward as Rupert in *Humpty Dumpty*. Palace Theatre, Belfast, 1907.

184. Dorothy Ward as Jack in *Little Jack Horner*. Theatre Royal, Manchester, 1910.

185. G. H. Elliott as Chocolate sings 'How d'you do, my lady?' with the Children. *Mother Hubbard*. Prince's Theatre, Bristol, 1909. 'The Chocolate-Coloured Coon' of the music halls written into pantomime as an Indian servant!

186. Tom Foy as Idle Jack. *Dick Whittington*. Shakespeare Theatre, Liverpool, 1909.

187. Carlton as Bison Bob in *Humpty Dumpty*. Prince's Theatre, Bristol, 1906. A music hall conjuror introduced into a pantomime in a written-in part.

188. Lily Morris as Colin in *Mother Goose*. Prince's Theatre, Bristol, 1905. 'Hear the Pipers calling Jenny mine.' Principal boys were very fond of kilts for their patriotic songs. 'The Scotch moors' or 'The Waterfalls of Scotland', with or without the Dagenham Girl Pipers, are still a 'stock' scene.

189. Harry Lauder as the Page (Buttons). *Cinderella*. Royal Court Theatre, Liverpool, 1907.

190. *Mother Hubbard.* 'On the Scotch Moors'. Prince's Theatre, Bristol, 1909.

191. *Mother Hubbard* 'The Fairy Dell'. Prince's Theatre, Bristol, 1909.

192. Walter Passmore as Reggie and Agnes Fraser as Robin Hood. *Babes in the Wood.* Drury Lane, 1907.

193. Dolly Castles and George Graves as Jack Halleybut and Mrs Halleybut. *Jack and the Beanstalk.* Drury Lane, 1910.

194. Johnny Danvers as King Rat-a-Tat II. *Jack and the Beanstalk.* Drury Lane, 1910. The last of the pantomime 'Triumvirate' of the nineties, with Leno and Campbell who had both died in 1904.

195. Fanny Fields and Malcolm Scott as Gretchen and Widow Twankey. The Laundry scene. *Aladdin*. Adelphi Theatre, 1907. The usual part of Wishee Washee here altered to suit 'Happy' Fanny Fields, a music hall comedienne who sang songs in broken Dutch.

196. Millie Legarde and Sarah Vrubell as Aladdin and Princess So Shi. *Aladdin*. Adelphi Theatre, 1907. Few oriental concessions seem to have been made in Aladdin's costume, which might well be for Prince Charming!

Opposite
197. *Cinderella*. Adelphi Theatre, 1908. Marie Rignold, Mabel Russell and Fred Leslie as the Ugly Sisters and Dandini. With a Dame (the Baroness) in the cast the Sisters were played by women with a male Dandini.

198. Dan Rolyat and John Humphrey as the Baron and Baroness. *Cinderella*. Adelphi Theatre, 1908.

199. Carrie Moore as Prince Charming. *Cinderella*. Theatre Royal, Birmingham, 1907. She played the same part in the Adelphi pantomime of 1908.

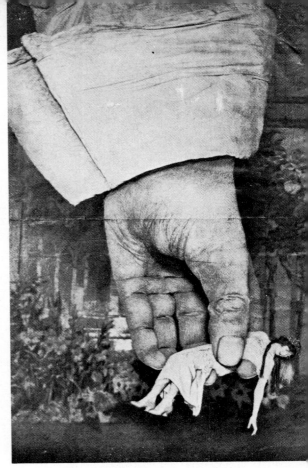

200, 201, 202. *Jack and the Beanstalk.* Drury Lane, 1910. Harry Randall as Prince Spinach 'Talks golf with the Giant'. 'The most remarkable feature of Drury Lane's pantomime, *Jack and the Beanstalk*, is the biggest of the giants, who is so large that he cannot be seen as a whole when on the stage. At one time his feet are visible to the audience; at another, one of his hands swoops down to pick up the Princess Dorothy (Julia James).' George Graves as Mrs Halleybut has trouble with 'The giant storks (the Pender Troupe), each carrying an egg in a nest'.

Opposite
203, 204, 205, 206. *The Sleeping Beauty.* Drury Lane, 1912. Florence Smithson as Princess Marcella (Beauty), Wilfrid Douthitt as Auriol (breaking tradition as a male principal boy), the Poluskis (Sam and Will), as the Detectives, Holmes and Blake (the traditional comedy 'duo', Brokers' men, Robbers or Captain and Mate). Will Evans, George Graves and Barry Lupino as Pompos, the Duke of Monte Blanco and Finnykin. The next two seasons' pantomimes continued the story with almost the same cast: *The Sleeping Beauty Be-awakened* and *The Sleeping Beauty Beautified* (with Bertram Wallis as Auriol).

207. *Top Left*. Clarice Mayne as Aladdin. Theatre Royal, Leeds, 1913.

'There is a distinct tendency on the part of the modern pantomime boy to leave behind those traditions which prescribe for her wear tights and trunks. Here is a case in point, where we see Miss Clarice Mayne in one of the several dresses designed for her to don as Aladdin. So it is that the principal boy—the "nut" of pantomimes —progresses with the times.'

208. *Above*. Dorothy Ward in *Jack and the Beanstalk*. Palace Theatre, Manchester, 1920. The most famous of this century's principal boys, who continued to play 'Boy' to her husband, Shaun Glenville's, 'Dame' until Christmas 1957.

209. Ella Retford as Robinson Crusoe. Opera house, Manchester, 1926. Her 'Boy' career stretched from 1909 to 1949.

210. *Jack and the Beanstalk.* London Hippodrome, 1921. Clarice Mayne as Jack, George Robey as Dame Trot and the Penders as the Cow.

211. Nellie Wallace as Widow Twankey. *Aladdin*, London Hippodrome, 1920. One of the very few female Pantomime Dames.

212. The Dolly Sisters, Rosie and Jennie, in *Babes in the Wood.* New Oxford Theatre, 1921. C. B. Cochran's only excursion into the world of pantomime.

213. *Mother Goose*. London Hippodrome, 1924. Shaun Glenville as Mother Goose, Fred Conquest as Priscilla Goose and Wee Georgie Wood as Jack, about to enter 'The Hall of Gold'.

215. *Opposite*. Dorothy Ward and Arthur Conquest as Robinson Crusoe and Man Friday. Empire, Liverpool, 1930.

214. *Aladdin*. Dominion Theatre, 1930. Lupino Lane as Pekoe and George Atterbury as Bonzo.

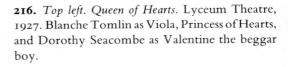

216. *Top left. Queen of Hearts.* Lyceum Theatre, 1927. Blanche Tomlin as Viola, Princess of Hearts, and Dorothy Seacombe as Valentine the beggar boy.

217. *Above. Robinson Crusoe.* Lyceum Theatre, 1930. George Jackley as Will Atkins, Constance Carpenter as Polly Perkins and Kitty Reidy as Crusoe.

218. *Dick Whittington.* Lyceum Theatre, 1925. Helen Gilliland as Dick, with Jack Hurst as Thomas the Cat.

Pantomime, in what became the traditional style, produced by the Melville Brothers at the Lyceum from 1910 until the theatre was closed soon after the 1938–9 production, changed little; old favourites either remained or returned and until the end a miniature Harlequinade concluded the performance.

219. Clarkson Rose as Mrs Crusoe who, from 1920 to 1967, was usually to be found somewhere each Christmas in drag.

220. *Top right.* Douglas Byng as the Queen in *The Sleeping Beauty*. A *grande dame* whose gallery of fine ladies stretches from 1924 to 1960.

221. George Lacy as Mother Goose. He first played the part in 1929 and continued to do so for the next eleven Christmases in London and the provinces. He has since played many other dames.

222. Fay Compton. *Dick Whittington*. London Hippodrome, 1932.

224. Evelyn Laye, Prince Florizel. *The Sleeping Beauty*. Theatre Royal, Birmingham, 1938.

223. Binnie Hale. *Jack and the Beanstalk*. Dr Lane, 1935.

225. Marie Burke, Robin Hood. *Babes in Wood*. Palace Theatre, Manchester, 1936.

26. *Cinderella.* Drury Lane, 1935. 'Love at First
ight.' Prince Charming and Cinderella, Phyllis
eilson–Terry and June.

227. *Beauty and the Beast.* Lyceum Theatre, 1937.
Jill Esmond as Prince Hal. 'She plays both parts—
save for a moment or two—and gives a pathetic
quality to the Monster.'

228. *Sindbad.* Theatre Royal, Exeter, 1933. Sindbad, Enid Lowe, carried off by the great Roc
with the assistance of the Spirit of the Waves, Adela Mavis, and the *corps de ballet.*

229. *Queen of Hearts*. Lyceum Theatre, 1933. 'The Castle of Cards', the famous collapsible set which is wrecked by the storm. It was used in three productions of the pantomime at the Lyceum in 1927, 1933 and 1938.

230. *Babes in the Wood*. Drury Lane, 1938. G. S. Melvin as Nurse Merryweather administering castor oil to the babes, Pat Warner and Beryl May.

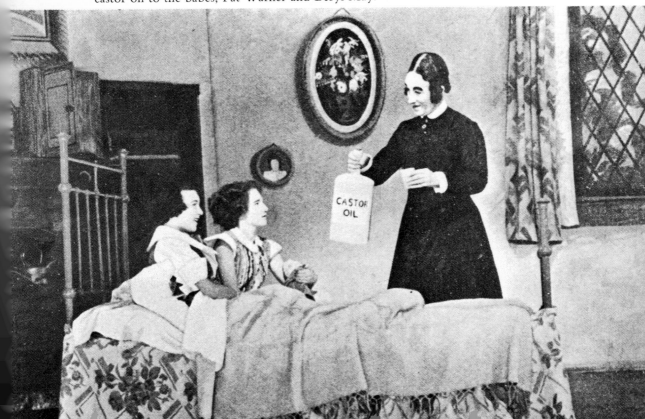

231. Pat Kirkwood as Prince Rupert. *Humpty Dumpty*. London Casino, 1948.

232. *Top right*. Carol Lynne and Arthur Askey as Cinderella and Buttons in the inevitable kitchen scene. London Casino, 1947.

233. *Cinderella*. Coliseum, 1939. Joan Cole and Patricia Burke 'as highly decorative and attractive principal boy and principal girl'. In spite of war and the black-out it was pantomime as usual, with a second generation principal boy.

234. Jimmy Jewel and Ben Warriss, as the Robbers, lead the children in a chorus song in *Babes in the Wood*. London Palladium, 1950.

235. *Cinderella*. London Palladium, 1953. 'The Palace of Porcelain'. The 'walk down'. Baroness Pastry (Cyril Wells), Baron Pastry (Richard Hearne), Prince Charming (Adele Dixon), Cinderella (Julie Andrews), Buttons (Max Bygraves), Buttercup (Jon Pertwee), Dandelion (Tony Sympson) and Dandini (Joan Mann).

236. *Cinderella.* Coliseum, 1958. The Richard Rodgers, Oscar Hammerstein II pantomime, with scenery and costumes by Loudon Sainthill, directed by Freddie Carpenter, which broke new ground with its integration of music, lyrics and decor in the musical comedy tradition.

237. *Aladdin.* Coliseum, 1959. The Finale of the pantomime from '*The Thousand and one Nights*', with lyrics and music by Cole Porter and a book by Peter Cooke. Directed by Robert Helpmann, with scenery and costumes by Loudon Sainthill.

238. Edmund Hockridge as Prince Michael (from the New World). *The Sleeping Beauty*, 'A Fairy Tale re-told'. London Palladium, 1958.

240. Jimmy Tarbuck as Jack in *Jack and the Beanstalk*. London Palladium, 1968. Tradition broken, the principal boy has become a singer, a 'Pop' singer or a comedian. The change began when Norman Wisdom played Aladdin at the Palladium in 1957. From then on the reign of the female 'Boy' ended in the West End of London.

239. Cliff Richard as Aladdin and Arthur Aske as Widow Twankey. London Palladium, 1964.

241. Dorothy Ward as Dick Whittington. Pavi Liverpool, 1957.

242. *Turn again Whittington.* London Palladium, 1960. Norman Wisdom and Yana as Dick and Alice.

243. *Puss in Boots.* London Palladium, 1962 Frankie Vaughan and Joan Regan as Francesco and Linda in 'The "Tale" of a Real Cool Cat'.

244. *Sleeping Beauty on Ice.* Empire Pool, Wembly, 1952. Daphne Walker skates as Prince Forthright with Gloria Nord as Princess Beauty. Since 1950 Gerald Palmer has directed a Christmas Ice Show at Wembley.

245. *Jack and the Beanstalk*. Theatre Royal, Exeter, 1955. Traditions remain outside London. The Ringmaster, Edward J. Wood, introduces a 'Speciality' The Delevantis, in the Fair Ground scene.

246. *Queen Passionella and the Sleeping Beauty*. Saville Theatre, 1968. A new version of an old story with Danny La Rue, in his fifteenth pantomime.

247. *Cinderella*. London Palladium, 1971. The Ugly Sisters, Teresa and Julia, Terry Scott and Julian Orchard. Dressed by Cynthia Tingey.

248. *Babes in the Wood*. London Palladium, 1972. Edward Woodward as Robin Hood. The National Theatre providing the latest principal boy.

249. Danny La Rue as Queen Charmaine, *Queen of Hearts*. Palace Theatre, Manchester, 1972. In a Mark Canter creation, directed by Freddie Carpenter.

DRURY LANE

CINDERELLA

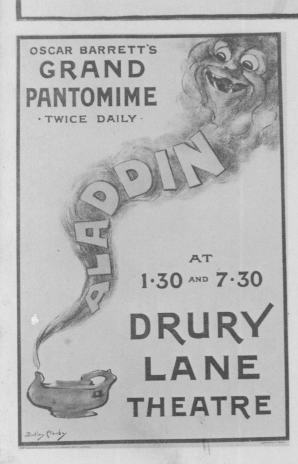

OSCAR BARRETT'S
GRAND PANTOMIME
· TWICE DAILY ·

ALADDIN

AT
1·30 AND 7·30

DRURY LANE THEATRE

DRURY LANE Pantomime

BLUE BEARD

Written &
Invented by ARTHUR COLLINS & J. HICKORY WOOD